one

last

kiss

Surviving the Death of My Spouse:

A Young Father's Story

Keith Leust

ISBN: 978-1-7324727-1-6

Printed in the U.S.A.

dedication

This book is born from an extraordinary life experience.

To Joannie my first love and late wife, a beautiful woman with a gentle soul who was not ready to go. She fought death so that she might live on with me and our boys.

Cancer took her, but my boys and I persevered. The journey was fraught with pain, gut retching loss and sorrow. In spite of it all, our boys and I survived, and have become more for the experience.

It is with great humility and a profound love that I thank and honor my current wife, Amy, for her help in coping with the pain of a devastating loss and for also lifting my heart to love again.

Amy is my sweetie pea.

Amy has embraced my boys and me. Together we are a family. Thank you, sweetie, for bringing back my romantic smile.

And to my boys, Andrew and Alex, who have walked beside their Dad. Together we have become stronger and more resilient. Together we have learned that life is a journey and no matter what we will support and love one another.

Finally, to the Lehman family, who lived, loved and lost with me. Their kindness, resilience and love helped us all endure and find peace. We have all been touched by Joannie and are more for her love.

I love you all.

- Keith

contents

foreward

*"Death is not the greatest loss in life.
The greatest loss is what dies inside
us while we live."*

~ Norman Cousins

In the summer of 2002 my wife, Joannie Leust, was diagnosed with breast cancer. Two years later I was standing at her casket.

The most beautiful woman I had ever met in my life was gone.

This is the story of what my wife, our children, family, friends and I learned about one another, ourselves and life along the way.

This is my story. These are my words. My experience. What I saw. Felt. Experienced.

The kisses that I gave. The prayers that were ignored.

I played a unique role trying to keep the family from imploding. From keeping Joannie losing hope. From our boys being crushed. Me from breaking.

I learned that nothing is grittier in its reality and more challenging in its texture than the fight for life. Unfortunately, cancer has become all too common, and in spite of amazing advances in medicine; people still die.

This is the heart-wrenching and inspirational saga of how my young wife battled breast cancer for two years. She taught us all on how to live, how to fight and how to die.

With dignity.

Her spirit and humility undergirded her losing battle which made it all the more poignant. During those two years she and I had tremendous support from family and friends; defining the essence of what those two types of relationships were eternally intended to be.

Unfortunately, when the grueling emotions and unrelenting tears made those last two months crawl by ever so slowly, we were not prepared for the abruptness and finality of the end.

That stunning denouement landed coldly and without warning like a giant fist to the stomach.

It left me and our two children emotionally gasping for air. My wife and their mother was the charming and powerful glue that held us all together.

As a family, we were forced to learn how to endure, grieve and finally move on together. In the end we learned the hardest lessons of all; how to begin to accept loss and how to celebrate life.

We would have made her proud.

One moment there was life, hope and a prayer. Then in an instant life was gone leaving us, the survivors with a final belief.

Joannie was an active participant in dying, up until her final breath. She never shirked from it, nor did she fear it. Instead, she participated in life in her own amazing way, as if to say,

> *"As long as I am alive; I will enjoy the riches of a life created by my Father in heaven."*
>
> *~ Joannie Leust*

She brought happiness, hope and a soft spirit to all that knew her and all that she touched. She not only shined her light on life; she brought us all the bright side of death.

In her mind, both were equally miraculous for they came from something much more than we can ever imagine. A force that binds the universe together.

> *"Life is a sea of vibrant color. Jump in."*
>
> *~ A.D. Posey*

She was, and I did.

That was my Joannie. She was my life.

introduction
How I Came To Be A Survivor

*"Hope smiles from the threshold of
the year to come, whispering it
will be happier."*

~ Tennyson

One day I woke up to a new life.

If you had told me that I would no longer be married and that I would have buried my wife, I would have believed you were crazy. In those halcyon days I had a beautiful wife, two wonderful children and a successful career.

All of my dreams had come true. In those twenty glorious years, life couldn't have been better.

Then in the summer of 2002; everything changed. Joannie was diagnosed with breast cancer and after a heroic battle she died two very short years later.

Just like that.

It was over.

I was alone.

A single dad with two young children.

"In the wake of sudden death 'normal' ceases to exist. I wasn't ready to say goodbye."

Her experience left me humbled. It also left me stunned, confused, lost, lonely and feeling powerless. I had helped my wife struggle against an overwhelming disease, as she vainly fought to live for, "just one more day."

We prayed, hoped, ached, mutually supported and passionately loved each other every hour of every day.

Ultimately, the disease proved too strong. In the end I found myself a grieving single parent of two young children. It was something I never imagined would ever happen to anyone I knew, let alone to me.

Is anyone ever prepared for an emotional event like this?

Never.

There is nothing like the finality of death in our human experience. Even when we know it is marching relentlessly to an uncompromising conclusion, that last breath can never be truly understood.

Until it is exhaled. Until the last breath is taken. Until the last kiss bestowed.

Joannie never gave up hope. She completely understood the disease she was battling, even as she lost a little bit to it every day.

My young wife was a warrior; she was not just fighting just for me as my wife but for our children as their mother. She truly believed it was not the time for her to die.

I knew I had married a beautiful woman. I had no idea she was a fiercely courageous one. Joannie took the lead in the confrontation with cancer. She was not going to go down easily.

When someone you love passes away it changes you. You are able to appreciate the nuances of your existence you never realized before. A death can awaken your life.

Each day is more precious than yesterday. The sounds you hear, the scents of the world and the possibilities of each moment are so much deeper than they ever were.

I feel fortunate for all that I have been given, and glad to have the strength to appreciate life as an unfolding adventure. I have come to accept that I actually control very little in life beyond my own response to everything around me.

I spent the first year coming to grips with grief; helping my children understand our new life as I slowly began to face my future without my Joannie.

"There is sacredness in tears. They are not the mark of weakness, but of power. They speak more eloquently than ten thousand tongues. They are the messengers of overwhelming grief, of deep contrition, and of unspeakable love."

~ Washington Irving

As I look ahead, I know that for me life is much fuller than it has been at any point in my life. I have witnessed and shared in a death that was full of grace. As a result, I have an incredible belief that there is much more to this life than I could have ever imagined before. It is with this hope and expectation that I greet each moment.

This is my saga. As with all great stories, it is not just about the tale but also about what happens next. The past years have been remarkable.

It is told from the perspective of a young father who struggled to help his wife survive. For two years I prayed that a miracle would come. Unfortunately, her death was neither my wish nor her hope.

In the end, I found myself a single parent with years of healing ahead of me.

Today I look at the world with a new appreciation. A respect for life that helps me remain humble.

I now have an understanding of how fragile the human condition really is and a belief that regardless of what life has in store for each of us, the journey, however wonderful or painful, will be remarkable.

Thank you for joining me.

transition

*"Other things change us, but we start
and end with the family."*

~ Anthony Brandt

This is about my late wife and the struggle that she fought so hard to win. To understand our family, I have included a bit more in this book.

To understand who we all are, as individuals, how we came to be a family, what our life was like before, during and after the battle with cancer I have added our history ... where it all began.

I hope that this provides a background, so you can appreciate the journey we took together.

In the End, it Starts with The Beginning

My name is Joan Leust – I am 44 years old. I am married to Keith; and we have two boys ages are 7 and 8. We live in Barrington, Illinois, about 40 miles northwest of Chicago.

The final chapter of my story began in late July 2002, when I felt a hard mass on the side of my left breast. I was going to my niece's wedding in Texas, so I asked my two sisters, both nurses; about the lump.

They said they were not sure, but to get it checked out...

chapter one

A Remarkable Girl

"Beauty is not in the face;
beauty is a light in the heart."

~ Kahlil Gibran

Joannie's parents were third-generation immigrants with roots in Europe. Her dad, "Big Al" Lehman, was of German descent and her mom, Carrie, was a mix of English, Scottish and a splash of German. Both their parents grew up in Brooklyn, New York, and moved to Haskell, New Jersey, to raise a family.

Haskell was founded in 1898 and was named for the Laflin & Rand Powder Company president Jonathan Haskell. They were a leading manufacturer of .30 caliber smokeless powder used in the United States Army service rifles until the mill ceased operations in 1926.

Why Big Al relocated his family in Haskell is beyond me.

Maybe it was for a reason as simple as finding work and it wasn't at the mill.

Al worked for over 40 years for ITT. He started out as a laborer in the union and after many years moved into a managerial position in the area of quality control.

At work he was known as one of the best people managers in the company; working with his staff to accomplish goals as opposed to "telling and managing them" to do what he ordered.

He was a natural leader. He loved people and they loved him.

Following his retirement, he and Carrie travelled the country for 18 months pulling a 40-foot trailer across as many States as they could. Then they bought a small home in Florida in a golf community and lived there for over 15 years, enjoying the beautiful climate and the good life.

Eventually, their health began to fail, and they moved back to New Jersey to a comfortable apartment where both of them passed away within a year of one another in 2011.

Neither Al nor Carrie went to college. However, as the respected patriarch Al made certain that each of his children graduated from college so that they would have a foundation to build their lives on.

Carrie was a full-time mom and raised nine children in a small three-bedroom house. Joannie's parents were "old school" and possessed the values and goals of their generation.

Joannie's siblings went into fields focused on helping others, nursing, insurance, human resources, aircraft consultant and a teacher. The youngest child, Mark, tragically died in a motorcycle accident at the age of 23.

The Lehman family of nine children was chronologically divided into two generations, five older children and four younger ones. Joannie was in the middle, the bridge between the two "families" keeping everyone connected right up to her death.

She was the glue that held everyone together.

A remarkable girl.

Growing up Catholic in the day when nuns used a wooden ruler to rap the knuckles of their wayward students. If you went to parochial school you are nodding knowingly here!

Nuns were tough. Maybe that's why their name rhymed with, "Huns," as in Attila.

A coincidence?

I would never mention that to them.

Not wanting to risk the wrath of God or her church, Joannie dutifully attended Mass every Sunday. When I asked her once, "Why do you go to Mass?" She frowned at me like I had the I.Q. of a kumquat and shot back, "Don't ask stupid questions; this is how it's done!"

Oh.

Ask a stupid question and pay the price.

Needless to say, my wife was a devout Catholic.

Joannie graduated from Montclair State University, the second largest college in New Jersey, with a Marketing Degree and worked for several large firms in New York City.

She took a bus each day to the Port Authority and for her morning exercise power walked over 40 blocks to the office.

Like I said earlier, *remarkable.*

chapter two
The Inventive Boy

"My interest in life comes from setting myself huge, apparently unachievable challenges and trying to rise above them."

~ Richard Branson

My parents were, 'off the boat.' My dad arrived from Germany at Ellis Island with his dad and sister in 1920. His mom had passed away when he was very young, leaving his father to struggle and care for their two young children.

There was little work to be had after World War I in Germany. My grandfather lived and died a sheet metal laborer.

But, his life was so much more than that of a factory worker.

Since he was unable to provide for my dad and aunt, he put both my father and Joan into an orphanage in New Jersey.

When they grew up, they both escaped from that abusive environment.

Joan, his sister, was 18, and my dad was 15, when they bolted for freedom. They had endured a childhood of hardships, abuse and neglect.

My father told the family that he started working when he was 15 years old as a delivery boy and finally got a part-time job at a dental laboratory, the field that he pursued throughout his life.

Knowing the importance of a high school diploma, he took evening courses to attain his GED. By the age of 21, he became a Freemason aspiring to follow the Order's decree for man's moral, intellectual and spiritual development.

He became an avid reader of Western and Eastern philosophy and science and had an endless thirst for knowledge.

My dad was truly a Renaissance man.

That influence rubbed off on me years later and continues today.

He spoke German and Spanish which helped him conduct business across Europe, Mexico and South America. He enrolled in business courses at the university and later attained a real estate broker's license.

Believing in the benefits of a holistic and sacred lifestyle and wanting to experience it, he went on a 10-day fast. My mom related that he returned with the clearest eyes and skin, relaxed and more handsome than ever.

My father was extremely handsome with movie star looks. He was developed into a sheet metal artist, able to make designs and castings in metals, including silver and gold and ended up in a large company doing dental and surgical research.

He was even selected to work with a New York City dentist to develop a new process; dental implant technology in the 1950's, and became well-known at dental universities throughout the U.S.

My father was a remarkable human being.

He was a humble, gentle, spiritual man; never mean, loved us truly, and saved hard to make sure his children went to college. I never remember him scolding or yelling. He always came home with a smile and looked forward to being with us and being part of our growing up.

I never heard or saw my parents fight, they truly adored each other. He shared his knowledge and some of his life's experiences with us. He could be very social and funny, was adept at the piano and harmonica (he played them by ear!) loved the ocean and spent a lot of time at the beach.

I see a lot of myself in him and am proud to be his son.

My mother Anneliese, emigrated to the U.S. as well from Germany; enduring the horrors as a child in World War II.

She survived scores of bombings, hearing of people who spoke out against the regime being incarcerated including the day when she heard her mother being threatened by uniformed men to incarcerate her.

That terrified my mom to hear that her mother was threatened to be jailed for speaking out.

On a regular basis, she stood in line for hours with other children and adults, beginning at six o'clock in the morning; just for a quart of milk or a loaf of bread to help feed the family.

Mom experienced the loss of countless members of her family and was even strafed by a low-level allied fighter plane when she was nine years old, dodging its bullets everywhere.

My mother was a tough lady.

But she never gave up and always wanted something better than what she had lived through and witnessed during those days of injustice and inhumanity.

She persevered and survived; qualities that she instilled in me to this day.

"When the world says, 'Give up,' Hope whispers, 'Try it one more time.'"

~ Author unknown

She arrived in Hoboken, N.J., aboard the good ship New Amsterdam in 1955, as a 21-year-old with less than $40.00 to her name. Thanks to a friend's help in New York City, she was able to rent a tiny room at a Home for Single Women run by the Catholic Church for $8.00 a week, and a dinner for $1.00.

Luck would follow.

She had met the manager of an international company on board the boat who had given her his business card and suggested that she apply for a secretarial job. She began working three days later ultimately meeting my father at a Christmas party!

My strong-willed mother rose from being a secretary to eventually becoming a scientist at a large analytical instruments company. Her dream beyond getting a job was her passion to go to college.

She began attending classes went to Washington Irving evening high school to obtain the New York State Regent's English and American History certificate necessary to be able to matriculate at a college.

After she heard that as a full-time secretary at Columbia University one could get six credits free per semester, she applied and became a secretary for an English Professor. She took courses four nights a week, and ultimately enrolled at Hunter College full time and began working towards her Biology degree.

Money was getting tight, so she added a job at an investment counseling firm as office manager and was trained to become an investment counselor.

She married my father in October 1960, and finally received a B.S. degree in German History/Philosophy along with a high school teaching degree with honors.

A remarkable and resourceful woman.

I was born on the morning of July 23, 1961, in Yonkers, New York, and my two gorgeous and loving sisters would eventually follow.

My sisters and I were christened Catholic, but our family only went to church on holidays. Mom and dad were more spiritual than religious and believed the Ten Commandments were important as they lived their life according to their interpretation of understanding them.

But, their main focus was to learn how to become more aware in daily life; how to understand and participate in this world, and, how to honor our existence.

We never ate a meal without first closing our eyes and reverently being aware of sitting together as a family and being grateful for all we had.

Apart from my birth in 1961 it turned out to be a milestone year.

Baseball fans remember that was the torrid summer of Mantle and Maris and their hot pursuit of Babe Ruth's record of 60 home runs.

It was also marked the first year of President Kennedy's administration, the disastrous Bay of Pigs assault in Cuba, our first astronaut in space and the construction of the Berlin Wall.

Of course, the most important event in my life was breathing.

I was just happy to be alive.

If you know me today, you would not see much difference between my formative years and my current personality and set of values.

From what my mother remembers about me I was beautifully handsome with silvery blond hair, clear blue eyes, inquisitive, intelligent, cooperative, creative, inventive, somewhat introverted to the world outside, but always friendly and interested in participating in everything.

I'm not sure about the handsome and silvery part but, I still love people, am annoyingly inquisitive and being involved!

Growing up I loved to experiment with gadgets and technical innovations of all kinds. I am frankly surprised I survived my crazy explorations. I didn't always think through the consequences of my productions. I never knew it then, but nothing escaped my parents, I found out later that they were always looking to make sure I did not go too far.

Like the time I proudly constructed airplane wings. There was nothing wrong with the effort but the flaw in my concept was that I was the airplane. Those wings I made would have trouble holding up a moth much less a human being!

I climbed up on the roof of our garage and prepared to launch myself when my mother strolled out and looked up at me with a horrified expression on her face.

"Keith, what are you doing; you're not planning to jump are you?"

I calmly corrected her, "Oh no, mom; I'm going to fly!"

Within seconds she had me climbing back down off that

roof. My brief history as an airplane was thankfully short-lived.

My creative mind did not serve me well in school. At the end of the third grade I had a heart to heart with my parents, "I'm bored with school," I informed them.

They immediately took action.

From grades 4-8, I was enrolled in an academically challenging Montessori school where I thrived in class. Those were key learning days in an environment that stretched me in wondrous ways.

In my private time I was always building structures. I would have made a good architect.

I even revamped our frozen driveway with more cold water and built a toboggan track to zoom into the neighbor's yard. I constantly explored acres of farmland across the street with my sister Annette, my cohort in many an adventure.

She was only two years younger than I and we were like peas in a pod, most of the time!

I would climb trees and create little houses and getaways. I loved water, any body of water, and spent days figuring out ways to make it part of my life.

At the age of four years, I fell out of our boat while my father was working on the inside. Luckily, he quickly realized I was missing and came out just in time as I bobbed up near the float and he rescued me. He immediately brought me into the house, put on a dry set of clothes in order to bring me out right away to avoid my being afraid of water forever.

I couldn't wait to get back out to the boat again. However, my father who always wished he could have lived on the waterfront; was scarred forever and never bought a house near the water again nor ever wanted a swimming pool.

My favorite place as a child was to visit my grandparent's farm in the country near Munich, Germany, riding in a tractor, playing in the meadows and the woods, swimming, wading and rowing in the brook on the property, catching frogs, picking and eating fresh carrots from Oma's garden, and spending lots of time with my numerous cousins.

It was heaven!

When I was ten years old we had planned a family vacation to visit with everyone, but then my father couldn't get away and the trip was cancelled. I was very disappointed, so my mother asked if I wanted to go *alone*.

Wild horses couldn't keep me back!

She booked the flight and that summer became my fondest memories as a child.

I was a little man with the body and mind of a boy.

Our parents gave my sisters and me the freedom to create and explore on our own. We were encouraged to be creative and artistic. As an esoteric family we studied everything from Aristotle and Plato to world religions and even reincarnation.

We didn't smoke or do drugs; instead we found inner peace and happiness through meditation and togetherness. We were working hard to discover who we were as individuals and as a family.

It was a very rewarding way of life.

Of course, I was also a normal kid. I mowed lawns, had a paper route and built a model airplane from a kit with my dad that crashed and shattered all over the street within moments of its launch.

Like I stated, I was a normal kid.

When there was a major eclipse of the sun my dad and I built a device to watch it so our eyes would be protected.

My mom and I built gingerbread houses for our family members and close friends.

My sisters Annette and Astrid, and I were always involved in a myriad of projects whether it be kitchen duty, cooking, cleaning, ironing, it was expected that we have these skills. We even painted the outside of our house several times, of course the rooms also.

Once I made a hole in the wall of my bedroom because I wanted to know what was behind it. My mother also was curious and since the area seemed large and empty, she suggested we open the hole further, which resulted in me getting an additional closet which my father and I built together!

My mother had a large organic garden and we were involved in planting, mulching, picking corn, string beans, tomatoes, etc., We even had a stand at the end of the driveway to sell some of the vegetables. (Mostly to keep us busy!)

We had a mixed lab and shepherd dog named Penny. She

even picked her own corn, tomatoes, raspberries, apples which also typified our later dog, a white shepherd named Susha.

Everyone was always part of everything, including our pets.

Build, build, build… study and work … that was my life.

I even took piano lessons for ten years and practiced most every day, also did recitals. Mom even bought a Steinway built in the 1890's from an Austrian opera singer. I had it completely rebuilt recently and now it is in my living room. My youngest son Alex loves to play his own compositions, just like my father.

I had little time for friends or a social life. I had not even discovered girls by the age of fourteen. I loved to read, still do.

Then came high school and everything changed.

I made strong friendships with others who shared my inventive passions. It was nice to be part of a group instead of always having to create things alone.

And, I fell in love.

Her name was Denise. She was my first girlfriend. It didn't end well and I was devastated when she broke it off. I swore off girls for a long time. The pain scarred my heart in ways that have remained.

And, so it goes with young love.

It was time to attend college. I had to pick a major. My dad and I talked, my mother suggested architecture, my father engineering. He felt that a job as an architect would be unpredictable, depend on the economy, while as an engineer you can do most anything anytime and always get a good paying job.

chapter three
Keith: The College Years

"College is the best time of your life. When else are your parents going to spend tens of thousands of dollars a year just for you to go to a strange town and get drunk every night?"

~ David Wood

Going away to college as the first born son of an immigrant family was an honor and a great responsibility for me. I was expected to be more than what my parents had achieved.

This was not going to be easy.

Going to Lehigh University in Bethlehem, Pennsylvania, and studying Engineering was not the problem. It had one of the finest Engineering schools in the nation, the P.C. Rossin College of Engineering and Applied Science.

Wonderful.

It also had a reputation as one of the top party schools in America.

Scary. Exciting. Intriguing.

This brought a big-time temptation into my sphere of hard work and accomplishment. My focus was going to be distracted, to say the least!

Lehigh had a healthy Greek system. Almost every night a fraternity party could be found on the "Hill" where the fraternity houses were located.

Free beer flowed well into the morning hours especially on the weekends. It was not uncommon to see students walking back to their dorm room while others were passing them on the way to breakfast.

As a freshman I was dropped into this environment and naively embraced the distractions of free beer and parties with reckless abandon.

My mother remembers with horror the day when they brought me to Lehigh. She saw that a driveway to a frat was filled with tables and kegs of beer.

She frowned at me and asked, "Is this an omen?"

I spent my fair share of nights dancing, laughing and just having fun with all my new friends. We all had nicknames thanks to our fellow dorm room friends.

Given how I embraced the wilder side of Lehigh University,

I was named "Shots." It had a double meaning for me. Yes, I could drink slugs with the best of them and as a child I had spent summers on my grandmother's farm in Germany where I was called Shotzie.

So, there you have it!

In spite of all my fun, I graduated as planned with one delicious diversion. I spent my fall semester during my senior year at the University of Salzburg as part of an exchange program.

This proved to be a complete liberation from the science and math that I had been immersed in for the first three years at Lehigh University.

Joyfully, I was back in my family's culture, listening to and speaking German, visiting with relatives. I was able to explore a very different side of myself.

I was not focused on math and science; but culture, language and art. I was exposed to beauty that I had never imagined, taking in the Mona Lisa at the Louvre, seeing the classic statue of David in Florence, exploring the back canals of Venice.

Granted there was beauty in math but that was black and white compared to the kaleidoscope of colors from the great artists and sculptors!

These creative geniuses transcended numbers and formulas. Each day of my semester abroad brought new tastes, sights and experiences that I still value decades later.

In all candor, what I learned and experienced in six months

in Europe eclipsed what I spent in a classroom in $3\frac{1}{2}$ years at Lehigh University in Bethlehem Pennsylvania.

You just cannot underestimate the imaginative beauty of man's mind.

chapter four

A Young Man on a Mission

"What lies behind you and what lies in front of you, pales in comparison to what lies inside of you."

~ Ralph Waldo Emerson

I graduated from Lehigh University in Pennsylvania with a B.S. in Engineering and began my career. I went on to earn two Master's Degrees which helped advance my opportunities.

I began my career as an engineer at ITT in New Jersey, like my father-in-law. I spent seven years working for ITT and American Express before I joined Arthur Andersen in 1990 to do management consulting.

In 2000, I relocated my young family, Joannie, and our two boys, Andrew and Alex, and took a job working for Motorola in Illinois. I rose to the position of senior executive in Human Resources and even ran Motorola University for several years.

In addition, as the first born in the family I was the designated heir to my father's legacy. I was responsible for the provision and protection of the three remaining women in our family.

My mom, and my sisters Annette and Astrid.

This was a heavy onus that overwhelmed me at times.

You never want to disappoint your Dad.

He was old school, traditional and from a proud heritage. I was more than a little conscious of the expectations he placed upon me from my childhood on.

To live up to a traditional European father was very serious business. In fact, he lingered on his death bed until I was able to show up and say goodbye to him.

He finally died on my birthday. I don't think that was a co-incidence. I believe that was willful. My father wanted me to take up his life as he ended it on the day I had started mine.

I was always my mother's go to person; but, I was my father's son.

I think about him every day.

By the time he passed away he left me in a good place in life. I will always be thankful for that. I will do all I can to carry on the Leust name with pride, dignity and honor. I would make my father proud.

I loved him very much.

chapter five
Meeting Joannie

*"I will find you. In the farthest corner,
I will find you."*

~ Mary E. Pearson

It was the mid-1980's and President Reagan was mired in the Iran-Contra scandal, Microsoft had just introduced a new computer concept called, "Windows," Chernobyl was melting down and, Madonna was prancing around like the virgin she wasn't.

I was single and looking for love in my own logical way. Then, I got lucky.

Several of us from work headed to a local watering hole which was featuring, "two for one" drinks. There, I ran into another co-worker named Sharon who did a wonderful thing for me, "Keith, I'd like you to meet my sister, Joannie!"

I took one look into her big, brown eyes and that was it.

My life had just been changed forever!

We spent the next four hours huddled in a corner in our own private world. We just talked and talked and talked some more. We couldn't get enough of each other.

We met for dinner a few days later and before I knew it we were meeting several times a week. We were falling in love.

"When two souls fall in love, there is nothing else but the yearning to be close to the other. The presence that is felt through a hand held, a voice heard, or a smile seen.

Souls do not have calendars or clocks, nor do they understand the notion of time or distance.

They only know it feels right to be with one another."

~ Lang Leav

On Friday nights I would head up to her parent's house where she was living to take her on a date. Most evenings when I pulled up the driveway I could hear a raucous party going on in their backyard.

Joannie was anxious to get out of the house and escape the asylum.

I was just as eager to find out what was going on in the backyard.

What I discovered in that backyard was amazing.

Her dad, Big Al, was holding sway at the gas grill; flipping burgers and cooking hot dogs. Next to him was a barrel of beer in a tub of ice. And, in the yard, was a volleyball net with at least a dozen people flailing away in a highly competitive game.

There were shouts, insults and people talking smack. I thought I had stumbled into an NBA playoff game. As the beer was consumed, the laughter grew louder and louder.

"*One Flew Over the Cuckoo's Nest* " had nothing on these people.

Most of the folks were her immediate family and close friends just having fun together. When you have a family of nine adult children there was a party every time they got together!

For me, growing up with just two sisters and no relatives to speak of, this was heaven. It was like attending a barbecue inside a video game while on vacation.

I *loved* her family.

I was quickly adopted by Joannie's parents and siblings They were a group of people who had a heart with enough passion to light up Atlantic City!

They celebrated each day like New Year's Eve was a *daily* event. Hence, our infamous limousine excursion...

During the Christmas holidays we rented two 40-foot limos, stuffed them full of people, food and plenty of drinks; and headed to New York City.

For six hours we drove around Manhattan and enjoyed a party on wheels. We would stop periodically so people from one limo could jump into the other one and vice versa. We were a mobile event happening that loved *variety*!

We took a nature break at the Plaza Hotel on the south side of Central Park and over 20 people blasted out of the two limos. We swarmed the hotel lobby overwhelming the staff as we raced to the bathrooms.

Arriving in limos at different venues made everyone believe we were rock stars! We came across as a whirlwind of star power. Even the crazy people in the City seemed tame compared to us!

Having grown up in very modest families, Joannie and I loved this celebrity fantasy. She pretended she was the rich and eccentric Lovey Howell, from Gilligan's Island, impersonating the quirky character's voice all night long and waving her hand at the crows who would gawk at us as we drove by.

Yes, the crows.

You have to be FEARLESS and take chances. Don't live life fearing what comes next. That's not what living is all about.

To drive home that point...

At her sister's wedding Joannie wore a strapless black dress that shocked her own mother! I thought she looked great in it.

Joannie was never afraid to take risks. She was her own person.

That was her family; open, caring, crazy and generous. And, I was fortunate to be a big part of their lives.

I had hit the jackpot with Joannie and my search for a partner was rapidly coming to an end.

And, I was joining a family that amped up my safe approach to life and made me realize there was so much more to my existence.

chapter six

Joannie: Who She Was

A woman's beauty comes in various shapes, sizes, textures and types. In Joannie's case she was aptly named.

She was a, "Joannie," not a stable Joan or a dependable Joanne; she was bubbly, effervescent, electrifying, magnetic and fun!

A Joannie.

She was as gentle as a feather flitting in the breeze, as feisty as a filly on the open track, as self-confident as a winning politician on election night, as selfless as server in a soup kitchen, as refreshing as light rain on a spring day, as trusting as a child when a stranger asked for help and as warmly intimate as the Best of Bread album.

If she was your guest at dinner she would be the first one to jump up at the end, clear the table and begin doing the dishes.

If someone felt uncomfortable in a crowded room she would sit down with them and make them smile.

If a neighbor needed help of any kind she was the first on their porch to fill their need.

My sister, Astrid, stated it best when she said, "Joannie was the last person who would ever come down with cancer; she was so full of life and love."

My wife seemed to have the ability to live forever.

She was one of those girls that one could never imagine that cancer could possibly happen to her. Vibrant, charismatic, luminous and possessing a presence of invulnerability.

Joannie did more than remember everyone's birthday she made sure it was a day of special honor for them. She made everyone feel happy they were alive.

Her time, energy and commitment belonged to the world she lived in. Joannie was not just a volunteer or a friend she was a memorable occasion.

Everything seemed to be in black and white until she walked in the door and then a kaleidoscope of COLOR!

She just had that way with people. She just lit up our world.

Yet, with all she meant to so many of us her dreams were simple and personal. She just wanted to have a great family which included me and our boys and our extended clans.

It was always Joannie that brought us together and made us close. We were her oxygen that fueled her familial passion and she was our holiday spirit!

She was a devoted Catholic and as ethical and moral as Jesus. She could be crazy and funny and wacky and she could also be a savvy promotions and marketing professional.

Joannie was all about people. She was all about life.

And, we were all blessed beyond measure to know her and love her...

chapter seven
Meeting My New Family

"Your girlfriend's sibling or parents might be totally nuts, but always defend them. Always. All a girl wants to do is to get along with her family and if you are on the side of making it easy, you will be loved eternally."

~ Mindy Kaling

Meeting Joannie and her family was a shock to my system! They were as crazy as I was predictable.

I was enthralled with their family and personal freedom. I liked life; they LOVED it! They did everything to the max and I hopped on their bandwagon of joy!

They say, *"Opposites attract"* and that adage was certainly true in my experience!

This family was charmingly nuts. Every day was New Year's Eve, The Fourth of July and even Halloween! They didn't just live life, they *luxuriated* in it!

The Lehman's embraced life like there was no yesterday, today or tomorrow.

This clan knew how to drain every drop of their existence in the most enjoyable and memorable way possible.

We smiled. We laughed. We did outrageous things. Each day was a celebration. We hugged one another and were thankful for being part of one another's lives.

I loved hanging out with them. I had never been around a family like theirs in my lifetime.

And, Joannie was at the center of their madcap antics always leading the charge and making her fun-loving father and siblings proud.

My quieter German upbringing was ignited by an explosion of crazy characters and colorful events.

It never mattered where we were or what we were doing or whether it was downtown Manhattan, the beach or an amusement park, the fun and laughter were a non-stop joy-ride.

In fact, this family was the amusement park. The gates were open 24/7 and the admission was free as long as you were willing to be yourself and not hold back in any way.

The Lehman's were GO time!

"Life is to be enjoyed not just endured."

~Gordon B. Hinkley

I knew after getting to know them my life would never be the same. I will love them forever.

I learned that the quietly determined and focused Keith Leust had a fun side and it balanced me out in a healthy way. I relaxed around them and it was simply marvelous.

Life is too short to just live it like everyone else. Goals, responsible work habits, accomplishments and successes are not substitutes for an invigorated soul.

I am a better person today because of Joannie and her family. My parents taught me how to conduct myself as a gentleman. Her family showed me how to have fun as a gentleman!

Or, at times; just have fun. I hope anyone reading this also has an individual or friends that teach you crazy.

It's the best.

My mother remembers well the first time I introduced Joannie to my family. She can still see her sitting on the couch, nicely dressed with a constant beautiful smile and those beautifully clear brown eyes looking right into you, very bubbly and talkative.

There was no tension, Joannie became quickly familiar to everyone at first acquaintance, just like meeting an old friend and spending the afternoon talking about this and that.

My father instantly liked and, as was his way, he had a multitude of questions, passionately intended to get to know her.

In the end, he thought her a wonderful match for me and was so very happy for us when we got married. He always wanted the best for me.

chapter eight
The Proposal

"The most crucial thing to know about true love is that it is not something you can find, rather you need to build it with the person in whose eyes you see your soul."

~ Abhijit Naskar, The Bengal Tigress

I took Joannie to one of her favorite restaurants in the Greektown section of New York City. I was so worried about losing the engagement ring that I attached it to a necklace around my neck!

Granted, I never wore necklaces, but I was afraid that the ring would somehow fall out of my pants pocket and get lost. So, that night, for the first and only time in my life, I wore a necklace!

At dinner I ordered an extra glass of wine for confidence

and excused myself so that I could use the washroom. Once there, I took the ring off the necklace and held it tightly in my hand.

When I returned to the table, I knelt on one knee next to her chair, looked up at a stunned Joannie and asked her, "Will you marry me?"

She was stunned because she had almost reached a point when she thought this moment would never arrive. She had been waiting for this moment forever, thanks to my methodical process of decision-making.

But, the time was right.

As I looked into her eyes I knew that we were meant to be Keith and Joannie Leust. This was the woman I could not live without.

Our marriage was more than two people committing to one another, being together in every aspect of life and creating a beautiful family.

For me this was emotionally overwhelming as I felt a tremendous responsibility to be the man Joannie was entrusting her life to; and thrilled beyond belief that she was exactly what I wanted as a lover, soul mate, best friend and wife.

I had always dreamed of being married to a woman that I trusted, cared for and loved (*in that order*) so that we could raise a family (together) and experience the excitement, joy, pain and satisfaction of being together.

I had waited a long, long time for this moment. But, that night as I knelt before the woman I loved, was worth waiting for. I felt like I had finally come home.

chapter nine
Wedding Bells

*"When you realize you want to spend
the rest of your life with somebody, you
want the rest of your life to start as
soon as possible."*

~ From the movie, "When Harry Met Sally"

We were married in a chapel in Joannie's hometown. Somehow, we fit over 150 people into a chapel that was designed to hold half that number!

It was a very 1980's Catholic wedding. My Joannie wore a white dress with a veil and looked stunningly gorgeous as she walked down the aisle. Of course, my best man, Heinzy and I had to play a prank during the ceremony just to shake up the troops.

We pretended we couldn't find her wedding ring.

After several moments of this contrived drama and a few glares from my future wife we laughingly produced her wedding band and everyone in the church breathed a sigh of relief.

Just having a little fun, that's all; a trait I had learned from *her* family!

As a couple we paid for most of the wedding costs. We were in a position to financially afford it and I wanted the best for her. It was high-maintenance East Coast replete with all the trimmings including a reception that knocked it out of the park.

That day I realized deep in my heart how committed Joannie was to be married to a man that she truly loved. A man that would honor and cherish her unconditionally. A man she could raise a family with together.

I was blessed to be that man.

I remember taking family pictures after the wedding. The Lehman's were so numerous the photographer had difficulty fitting all of them in the picture.

They crammed into every photo with over 30 people, all vying for their place in the group shot. Remember the U.S. hockey team after they received their gold medals at Lake Placid and they all crammed onto that small stand to celebrate?

That was the Lehman's at picture time!

Next came my family. There was, well.... my mother and father and two sisters.

That was it.

If the Lehman's were a small country, we were a closet.

But, we were proud to be forever linked to the Lehman clan and to have Joannie part of the Leust's.

We had hired a live band to provide music which allowed everyone to joyfully express their favorite dance moves. I remember my mom really kicking up her heels.

I tried not to stare. My God, it was my mother!

She was a 10 on *'Dancing with the Stars'*. No doubt.

At one-point, Joannie went to the washroom for a quick break and ran into my mom. My new wife commented on how impressed she was with my mom's dancing skills, to which my mother replied with more than a little confidence, "still waters run deep."

When she told me what mom had said I couldn't stop laughing!

My mother was just doing what came naturally to her, enjoying the moment and letting her emotions and in this case, feet, just have fun.

Anneliese Leust was one of a kind!

Our honeymoon was magical.

We spent ten days in Hawaii. We did a lot of sleeping in and loved having breakfast at 10:00 am every morning.

Honeymoons are special.

We walked the beach. We danced. We explored.

One of our greatest memories was taking a van to the top of Mt. Haleakala and then riding bicycles to the bottom of that 10,000-foot volcano.

The day started early, with a van picking us up at 3:00 am in the morning.

We were driven to the top of the volcano in time to see the sunrise. We were up so high that the sun came up over the clouds which were below us at around 7,000 feet!

It was amazing to see the sun slowly climb over the horizon, its colors exploding in the crystal-clear air. As the sun emerged the 100 or so folks who were there to welcome the new day started applauding God's handiwork of nature.

It was a moment that I will forever hold dear.

With the sun fully in the sky we each were given a mountain bike and we began our descent. It was one long ride to the bottom of the volcano. There was no pedaling required!

The best part was biking through the clouds.

The mist swirled around us as we passed through them. I cannot do verbal justice to the feeling of those moments. We descended until the jungles of Hawaii became clearer.

We neared the end of our trek and finally stopped at the Maui Lavender Café for a fantastic breakfast. Everyone was smiling and laughing. It was such a powerful and positive experience.

I remember feeling so alive. Joannie was beaming. We had just seen the sunrise, biked through clouds and had something to remember for the rest of our lives.

Every day was colorful. We swam on beaches covered in white, green and black sand. We held each other tenderly all night long and smiled warmly when we woke up.

We totally experienced the essence of being a couple. We held hands. We laughed together. We said and did whatever we wanted and our free-spirited love for each other brought us even closer.

There was nothing and no one more important than Joannie. I adored her. Each day was a new exploration in the wilds of Hawaii and a new experience in the knitting of our souls.

To see her smile, to laugh, to purr made me realize I was the most blessed man on earth.

More importantly, it became clear to me that, "I was her husband."

That is a wonderful moment, men.

chapter ten
Husband and Wife

"Compromise, communicate, and never go to bed angry – the three pieces of advice gifted and re-gifted to all newlyweds."

~ Gillian Flynn, Gone Girl

Joannie and I dated for several years before I finally popped the question. I may move slowly, but I've never been late yet!

She had a far different DNA; Joannie was more than ready for a commitment, I on the other hand was very happy simply being in a relationship with her.

I was an emotional crock pot and she was a romantic microwave.

Eventually, my mind reasoned that I couldn't live without her.

Looking back, it is clear that while I was always fully committed to her, I was afraid of what the commitment of marriage would be like in reality.

Granted, it was an irrational fear on my part, but it prevented me from marrying this wonderful woman sooner.

Fortunately, Joannie was a woman of great patience and once we were married life became even fuller. I had truly found a life partner, someone to share all of my life's experiences with and to plan a fulfilling future.

Our life was full, had wonderful friends and our individual families lived close enough for us to see as often as we liked; but not so close that they were involved in every aspect of our lives.

In time we bought a small house and began to make plans for our own family. One of the reasons I asked Joannie to marry me was because I knew that she would make a great mother. She had a heart as deep as the sea and the patience of a saint.

Every time she saw a baby or young child she would smile and make cooing sounds to the infant. Joannie had all the qualities a great wife and mother needed to possess.

I was a lucky man when she had agreed to marry me.

We were living the Dream.

I was a successful executive on the corporate fast track, working for companies like American Express, Prudential and Motorola. We managed our life and expenses wisely so that Joannie was able to be a stay-at-home mom.

My life was a fairy tale. I never imagined it would turn out as well as it had. I was the happiest man on earth.

chapter eleven
Parenthood

"Marriage teaches you how to compromise in life; children change your life!"

Both of us married fairly late in life. I was 28 and "Lovey" Joannie had just turned 30. We had dreams of starting a family but there seemed to be a problem. We had trouble getting pregnant.

Why does it take 50 million sperm to fertilize <u>one</u> egg? Because they won't ask for directions either!

All joking aside, our doctors told us that Joannie and I had medical issues which made pregnancy difficult. The medical experts figured out the problem and we put together a plan.

I had a varicocele procedure which required a small incision into the abdomen close to where the testicles originally descend through the abdominal wall. This allows for more sperm motility and increases the odds of me impregnating my wife.

Andrew was born naturally and on time. Unfortunately, complications at birth required him to remain behind and in the Neonatal Care Unit (NICU) for two weeks before he could come home.

Joannie was artificially inseminated which resulted in our first pregnancy.

We didn't stop there.

Since we were not getting any younger, we decided to proceed with a second pregnancy fueled by a second round of artificial insemination.

Joannie was again pregnant. A month later an excited doctor's visit announced that she was having twins!

We were overwhelmed. We were now on pace to have three children within 18 months. When you're hot you're hot!

Or, in theological terms; it was a miracle.

Then a new reality hit us right between the eyes.

At Joannie's two-month doctor's visit; tests revealed that not all was well. Because my wife was over 35 she had a test done to ensure the twins would be healthy.

The results were tragic.

Marissa was diagnosed with spina bifida and would die shortly after birth. Her twin brother, Alex, would be okay. I was on the road in Illinois and I remember getting a call, pulling me out of a business meeting.

My mom was on the other end of the line. She told me in a very concerned voice, "There's a problem with Marissa!"

My heart sank, "What kind of problem?" I asked her.

When I heard the words, "spina bifada". I felt helpless. Our little girl was fighting for her life. Joannie was in bed sobbing. I raced to the airport and took the next flight home.

As I walked in the door Andrew was excited to see me. I remember hugging him, thankful that he was part of our lives. As I held him in my arms, my thoughts were with Joannie, crying in bed, devastated with the news that one of her twins would soon die.

There were no guarantees with Alex, either.

I left Andrew downstairs with his grandmother and slowly opened our bedroom door. I immediately heard Joannie's whimpered cries quietly coming from our bed.

She was emotionally shattered. I had never felt more helpless in my life. All I could do was gather her in my arms and hold her tight.

We cried for hours. At that moment, my Joannie was carrying two of our precious unborn children.

One was destined to die. The other, if we were lucky, would live.

The horror inevitably began to unfold. At 28 weeks, Joannie went into premature labor. At that stage, neither child would have a fighting chance. Their lungs were not fully developed and living outside the womb was extremely tenuous, if not fatal.

Joannie was given a potassium drip, stopping her contractions. Over the next two weeks the doctors added steroids which were delivered to the twins to accelerate lung development.

The race was on to save their lives. We had limited resources and very little time.

Joannie was ordered to bed rest for the next two weeks. At that point, 30 weeks into her term, the twins announced themselves. Nothing was going to stop nature from taking its course.

It was time.

The twins were coming.

Even as I type this, I remember vividly sitting in a chair next to my wife and watching breathlessly at the orchestrated dance of the medical teams. They were flawless in their execution of professionalism under fire.

There were fourteen people in the room; two teams of 7, one for each child. As soon as each twin was born he and she were rushed out of the room for evaluation and critical care.

Within an hour, Joannie went from being pregnant with twins in a flurry of frenzied activity to suddenly sitting in a hushed room alone with me.

One moment there was a cacophony of noises and cries of medical staff shouting directives and the next minute there was an eerie silence as my wife and I looked strangely at each other trying to fathom what had just transpired and fearful of what was yet to come.

It was uncomfortably surreal. Everything had happened so fast our heads were spinning and then it was eerily quiet.

Only a parent with a deep and abiding love for his child would understand what I am describing here.

After a while, a doctor came in with the news, "Mr. and Mrs. Leust I have some news here. Your son Alex is going to be okay, but he will need extraordinary care for weeks to come."

We held our breath as he concluded his report remindful that we had a second child here.

His face was heartbroken, "We are bringing your daughter to you so you can say goodbye to her. I'm sorry."

My chest tightened up and I could feel a pounding in my head that was beyond unbearable. I sat numbly by as a nurse brought our Marissa into the room, all bundled up, and laid her on Joannie's chest.

Our little girl was beautiful. She looked like an angel.

And, within an hour that is exactly where she went to spend the rest of eternity with all of them, safe and protected in God's loving presence.

Marissa died in her mother's arms.

I remember every second of those fifty minutes. Those moments will forever be a part of me.

"In some aspects losing a child is like a wall, but instead of getting over it, you must carry the wall with you, wherever you go, for as long as you live."

~ John A. Passaro

Alex remained in the hospital recovering from his ordeal and fighting to regain his lungs while we attended the funeral of his sister. I remember to this day Marissa's casket.

It was just two feet long.

All three of our children's births had something in common; on the appointed day when babies are normally discharged from the hospital, none of them came home with us.

Joannie and I and our marriage never fully recovered from losing our little girl. She will always be with us in the most painful of memories.

chapter twelve
Family Over Career

"It's not hard to make decisions when you know what your values are."

~ Roy E. Disney

I remember a life-changing phone call one Sunday night from Joannie. She was sick and both our boys had a cold. I had been on the road for two weeks straight and was still with a client working late into Sunday evening.

This was the grinding existence of a consultant; not a life for a family man.

I thought about my wonderful childhood and how my parents were always there for me and I made some key decisions.

The next morning I was on a plane home and within a month quit and found a job with no travel. I was going to be home every night with my wife and kids.

I moved our family to a wonderful community northwest of Chicago and within a year Joannie was on a first name basis with almost all of the teachers in the elementary school and including the principal. Her focus was to be an active part of her boys' lives.

She had no aspiration to run the PTA unlike other parents, and firmly turned down the presidency when it was offered to her.

She just wanted to be a great mom.

I was the breadwinner of the family; Joannie was the stay-at-home executive; the constant caregiver. We were fortunate to be able to do this on my income.

It occasionally stressed me out, knowing that I was supporting a family of four plus a dog! But, my passion to be a great husband and father always won out through any bumps in the financial road.

I also found myself, along with the other husbands, revamping the streets and signs of our community. We dug post holes, painted, designed and spruced up our neighborhood all under the watchful eye of activist Joannie!

All the new signs were put up and I had dozens of new friends thanks to my people loving wife.

And, she didn't stop there.

When a mother in our community came down sick, Joannie arranged for the other moms to step in and help them by bringing meals to their families, transporting their kids to school and to extracurricular events and being surrogates in the familial ways.

That was Joannie; always taking care of the world. One child at a time.

Appropriately, when my wife struggled with her cancer, the other moms reciprocated. They were there for her in the same ways.

The dynamic presence of Joannie.

She even loved others when they had no desire to love her, or anyone else, back. We had a neighbor named Helen and on the woman's birthday Joannie walked over and gave her a modest gift to celebrate the occasion.

Helen responded back by saying, "Don't expect me to give you a gift for your birthday."

Joannie smiled and said, "That's fine, Helen. Happy Birthday!"

Every year my wife gave her friend a birthday gift and not once received any present in return. It never bothered Joannie. She didn't give things expecting to be reciprocated.

If she loved someone and wanted to make them smile on their birthday or any other day, she did so from her heart.

That was my wife.

This spirit of giving lit up our family life, too. Every year, the Lehman family went on a vacation to a house we had designated as our home away from home.

What a great time we all had!

Laughing, drinking, teasing, sunning in the sand and bonding as a family we loved. Of course, Joannie always organized the trip. She knew those times were going to be emotionally important for us to share together.

Joannie the glue.

I often thought to myself, "God help all of us if something ever happened to this remarkably loving woman."

Little did I know.

chapter thirteen

Bodily Betrayal

*"Sometimes something catastrophic
can occur in a split second that changes
a person's life forever."*

~ Jeannette Walls, Half Broke Horses

In April of 2002, Joannie had a mammogram and was told there was no problem.

Three months later, she felt a hard mass on the left side of her left breast.

Problem.

But, my wife couldn't believe it was serious.

She headed to Texas for her niece's wedding and while there she shared this latest development with her two sisters who were both nurses.

Mary felt the lump and got right to the point, "Go see a doctor as soon as you get home, Joannie."

My wife laughed and told her, "I just had a mammogram. I'm not worried."

Her sister frowned, "I am."

Now, my wife was concerned. As soon as she returned home she made an appointment with her primary care physician who ordered another mammogram and an ultrasound.

The mammogram cleared her again. But, the radiologist saw something suspicious there. Joannie asked him, "How suspicious?"

He chillingly replied, "I want to make certain it's not cancer."

Cancer?

By the time Joannie arrived home she was a nervous wreck. I arrived moments later when I heard her voice on the phone. I found her crying in our bedroom.

I was heartbroken.

I said to her, "Did the doctor say anything else?"

She said with voice trembling, "He wants to do a biopsy to see if…"

She couldn't finish the sentence. The reality of what might

be happening to her was already hitting home.

My God.

Joannie had the biopsy on July 5th and we waited anxiously for the results the following day.

The doctor called and told her, "You have ductal infiltrating carcinoma."

It is a cancer that begins growing in a milk duct and invades the fatty tissue of the breast outside of the duct. It is the most common form of breast cancer representing 80% of all breast cancer forms.

If diagnosed early on there is almost a 0% chance the patient will die. But, we were soon to find out a month later after Joannie's MRI that the cancer had already spread to her lymph nodes and it was a massive amount of disease.

The details of her diagnosis and treatment are explained clearly in Joannie's Journal in Chapter Sixteen.

For the next two years it was a living hell of hospitals, tests, treatments, prayers, good news, bad news, terrible news and finally the end.

It was like being on death row and waiting for the day of execution and hoping against hope there would be a reprieve from the governor.

But, no reprieve ever came for Joannie. It was just day after day of false hope and renewed dread.

I have never admired a human being more than I looked

up to her. She taught me about heroism, not in theory; but in real life.

Joannie Leust was the bravest person I have ever known.

chapter fourteen

Perspective

"Above all, be the heroine of your life, not the victim."

~ Nora Ephron

Finding out she had a potentially fatal disease caused my wife to reassess her perspective on life. Up to that moment of discovering the cancerous mass on her left breast, Joannie's life had been one filled with one joyous blessing after another.

She had come from a fun-filled family existence, married the man of her dreams, loved being the proud mother of two wonderful boys and was surrounded by great friends.

If a woman could have it all in life, Joannie Leust was living it.

Now, the focus and the challenge and the ominous reality

had darkly intruded into body, spirit and mind.

Where once there had been ongoing days of sunshine, there were dark clouds and a threatening sky with a perilous and powerful funnel cloud zeroing in on her.

There was no place for Joannie to go. The door to the tornado shelter was locked and she was trapped helplessly in the open air. All she could do was turn and face it and pray it would somehow pass harmlessly by her.

That is wishful thinking when it comes to the reality of cancer.

It is a misnomer to state, "you can fight cancer." There is no such entity. Cancer cannot be fought. The victim has no power against it. It is not a matter of the will. It is a series of medical and scientific treatments that either work or they don't.

Chemotherapy, radiation, stem cell treatments pound the patient in the hopes that the disease can be eradicated or stalled.

Joannie could only fight against her own fears and self-doubt. Her previous existence was now gone forever. She had to immediately adapt to a new way of thinking that was as scary as it was uncertain.

She was now in the battle for her life.

It was a fight in which she was more of a bystander than a participant. She had to keep her smile and trust her doctors and the treatments and hope for the best.

Up until the discovery of her cancer her days had been filled with marriage, motherhood, community activities, creative hobbies and fun with family and friends.

Now, her entire world was laser-focused on one goal.

Survival.

Unless you have cancer, you have no real idea what that feels like every moment of every waking day. Cancer dominates your thoughts, your bodily reactions and even your future dreams.

It is not just a crippling mindset, it is a relentless one.

If you break your leg or have a migraine, you know that pain and suffering will eventually abate, and you will be fine again.

But, it is unlikely that cancer will ever truly go away. Even when the victim is in remission there are a lot of sleepless nights wondering if it will return.

Joannie no longer had the luxury of being a heroine to the world around her, her husband, her boys, her family, her friends and her community.

She now had to learn to be a heroine to herself. That would be all she could handle here.

Her life had changed forever, and she knew it.

It was the scariest transformation I had ever witnessed in my life.

chapter fifteen

Joannie's Journal:
The Story in *Her* Own Words

*"Writing is the only way I have to explain
my own life to myself."*

~ Pat Conroy, My Reading Life

November 1, 2003

My name is Joan Leust – I am 44 years old. I have a husband, Keith; and we have two boys ages 7 and 8. We live in Barrington, Illinois, about 40 miles northwest of Chicago.

The final chapter of my story began in late July, 2002, when I felt a hard mass on the left side of my left breast. I was going to my niece's wedding in Texas, so I asked my two sisters, both nurses; about the lump.

They said they were not sure, but to get it checked out.

Over the next few days, my sister, Mary, kept insisting I go to the doctor. (Having felt the tumor, she had been more than a little concerned), so I went to my primary care physician. My doctor said she thought it was fibroids but told me to get a mammogram with an ultrasound. My last mammogram had been in April of 2002 which had proven to be negative.

So I scheduled my tests for Friday, August 2, with mixed results. The mammogram still did not indicate any problems, but the ultrasound *did*. The radiologist came in and told me my lump looked suspicious. That's when I heard the "cancer" word for the first time in relation to my body.

I do not remember anything else about the conversation because I could not get past the fact that I could have cancer. I cried all the way home and called my husband at work. Keith immediately came home and began calling various doctors for me.

Everything was so surreal; I was in a fog. I was terrified at the unknown.

I had my breast biopsy done on Monday, August 5, and I was completely consumed with the test; I could not think about anything else. I said so many prayers hoping it was not breast cancer.

The radiologist again told me it looked very suspicious, and would give me the results the next day. I knew then it was probably going to be bad news, and tried to prepare myself.

Well, as you can expect, one is never prepared for the phone call the next day, when they are told the shattering news. I had ductal infiltrating carcinoma, the most common form of breast cancer attacking 80% of its victims.

I was now an unfortunate statistic. The only thing I could do was cry!

How could I have breast cancer?

I was only 44 and had never felt so good in my life. I had lost some weight, and was working out regularly, but as I later learned, cancer affects all people, and does not have any criteria for choosing its next victim.

One thing became quickly apparent to me; I had to take next steps to figure out how do get this horrible disease out of my system, sooner than later.

There was no choice.

Cancer was not going to be my end.

My life depended on it.

My surgeon, Dr. Rosen, called me right after I spoke with the radiologist. He was so wonderful and understanding. He saw my husband and me that night and sat with us for about one hour. I memorized every word he said, studied his tone of voice and facial expressions to see what he thought my chances of survival were here.

He also took some liquid from my lymph nodes to find out if the cancer had spread. He suggested I go for a breast MRI at Lutheran General Hospital and he set everything up for me. I had that procedure done on Thursday, August 8. It had been less than two weeks since my lump had surfaced.

We were moving fast but would it be fast enough?

We met with Dr. Rosen the next day, and said there was too much cancer for a lumpectomy and suggested a mastectomy in my left breast. There was even worse news; the cancer had also spread to my lymph nodes.

I was so overwhelmed emotionally with this diagnosis. I also knew at that point I would need chemotherapy. They scheduled my surgery for August 20th and I also decided to do a bilateral mastectomy since I had a chance of it returning in my right breast.

Granted removing both of my breasts might only improve the odds of defeating this cancer by 5%, I was determined to do anything, everything to fight this disease.

At this point, I wasn't taking any chances. I was dealing with a fast-moving killer.

I did go to another surgeon for a second opinion, and he told me the same thing. He was also very competent, but I had a better rapport with Dr. Rosen.

I briefly considered going to Northwestern Hospital for a third opinion, but I knew they would not tell me anything different. It was now very apparent to me that my options were limited.

There was no denying reality. Cancer was now part of my life. I just had to figure out how to beat it.

When I talked with Dr. Rosen about the surgery, he suggested I get reconstructive surgery. It was my choice whether to do it at the same time as my breast surgery.

He suggested a plastic surgeon, Dr. Madry, whom I met about a week before surgery. I opted to get a TRAM at the same time as my surgery. The recovery time was only a week longer and I did not want to have to go back again for reconstructive breast surgery.

Two birds with one stone, right?

I also met with Dr. Tsarwhas, my oncologist, and he explained about chemotherapy, and he informed me that my treatment was dependent on how many lymph nodes had been affected.

He sent me for a bone scan/CAT scan to see if the cancer had spread to bones or organs. This was another traumatic event for me; the waiting was almost unbearable, but luckily the cancer had not spread beyond my lymph nodes.

I was so relieved!

"Sometimes even a small glimmer of hope can grow into a blinding light that shines on the entire world."

~ Susan Gale

All the doctors were in place and my surgery was scheduled. The weekend before the operation I went into the city with my family and tried to convince myself and everyone else that everything was okay.

But, in truth, I was still reeling from my diagnosis and second-guessing myself about a surgical procedure. At the time, I had questions; lots of questions.

"Is surgery right for me at this time?"

"Is my surgeon right about what he thinks I should do?"

"What will recovery be like?"

"How many lymph nodes are involved here?"

I instinctually knew the answer to all these queries. I was doing the right thing. My gut instinct was spot on here.

On August 20th I entered the hospital.

It was Showtime.

My operation started around 6:00 p.m. and I was wheeled out of the OR at midnight. I stayed in the hospital for another week. As a competitive person I was up and around the next day; not exactly running a four-minute mile, but I was at least walking around.

I had drains and a catheter and the good news was that the pain was not that bad.

But, there was bad news.

I found out that the cancer had spread to five of my lymph nodes forcing the surgeon to remove 14 of them. I came out of the hospital on August 25th and Dr. Rosen removed my drains which was a big relief for me.

My boys started classes on Tuesday, the 27th and I was

able to go to school with them and have breakfast with a few friends. Dr. Madry took my bandages off and told me how great everything looked.

Easy for him to say; I looked and felt like a scarred woman.

In a month, I had gone from a vivacious and healthy human being to a walking cancer stick. My breasts were gone. My life in the balance. This wasn't happening.

But, it was.

> *"Life is full of disappointments and setbacks. None of those things can permanently stop you. You have the power in you to overcome anything that life throws at you."*

Dr. Rosen gave me prescriptions for physical therapy and a wig.

I met with Dr. Tsarwhas on September 4th. Since I had cancer in five of my lymph nodes, I would have four treatments of adrymiacin/cytoxin and four treatments of taxol, with radiation after that.

Fasten your seatbelt, Joannie.

I would start chemo sixteen days later on Friday, September 20th. Cancer had punched first; it was now my turn to punch back.

I met with one of the nurses who told me what to expect

and what I needed to do before the chemo began. It was really important to have my teeth cleaned to get rid of as much bacterial as possible and go for an echocardiogram to make sure my heart was working properly, since chemo could cause serious stress on the heart.

Without wanting to, I was becoming a medical expert. This is cancer; it changes your entire life whether you are prepared for it or not. My tests began piling up. I was beginning to feel like a human pin cushion.

But, I wasn't complaining. My life or death was on the line.

I was going to live, my children were counting on me.

I was given information about side effects, prescriptions for anti-nausea medicines (both orally and rectally), and a thermometer to make sure that any fevers I incurred could be monitored, since the chance of infections are great when the immune system is compromised.

I also experienced cording syndrome under my arm, this is when the muscles fuse together tightly and have to be worked out with PT and daily exercise.

At the same time, I was measured for a sleeve on my left arm to be used in case of lymphedema, a condition of localized fluid retention caused by a compromised lymphatic system.

Cancer never plays fair. It hits you everywhere and is as relentless as a rampaging series of unrelenting waves battering the shoreline of our body.

You never know if you are coming or going. You never know

which aspect of it or the chemo itself will kill you.

Cancer moves freely, at will inside your organs, unseen in its discovery and unwavering in its march to destroy you.

No one is immune to its initial presence in your body.

It fires at will at either gender and cares not about race, religion, lifestyle, age, financial or social status, whether you are moral or immoral, in shape or unfit and maddeningly changes its pace at will.

Your main weapons of fighting it is surgery, chemotherapy, radiation; all crapshoots in their outcomes.

Each destructive in their treatment.

I had a few weeks before my first chemo treatment to ready myself for the side effects. I knew I would lose my hair so I went to the salon and had my stylist design a pixy-looking cut for me.

It was time to upgrade from the wig the doctor had given me. I went hair shopping. It was more than a little upsetting when I had to choose a wig in the first place.

I did not want to lose my hair and have to wear a wig; I just wanted to feel normal again! I did pick out a wig, but I never felt comfortable wearing it.

It wasn't me.

September 20th was my first day of chemo. During this time I was still continuing with my PT, and the cords in my arm were slowly being worked out.

I could finally lift my arm over my head; an accomplishment. Right after my surgery I went back to exercising. I started out slowly on the treadmill and worked my way up to speed walking. I felt so much better once I finished my exercise.

It definitely helped me heal quicker and gain strength. If cancer could talk, it would probably sneer at my efforts and mutter, "*Whatever.*"

I could not sleep the night before with the anticipatory dread of what was to come. My husband sat with me while the chemo was being administered. I was so thankful for him.

The Adriamycin was dark red and it made me sick thinking about this powerful drug bombarding my immune system having been inserted into the infusion port on my hand with a big syringe.

It felt like acid burning into my flesh as it coursed its way through my body. The pain was everywhere. I gritted my teeth, stayed my soul … I was going to beat this. No matter what it took, no matter what the pain. I was going to beat this.

I knew it was a non-negotiable in order to get better; but along with the bad cells, got the good cells, too.

Everything pretty much dies.

I was fighting to keep my *spirit* alive.

I had to keep telling myself that this was going to cure me; rid me of this toxic, deadly disease. After the Adriamycin, came the cytoxin, left jab and right cross.

Finally after 1½ hours I was done.

How did I feel?

Not so great the first night.

I took Zofran, which made me queasy, but I never actually got sick, not once during my chemo treatments. I settled into my first weeks of rhythm.

As if getting pumped full of toxic drugs could be called a rhythm.

I started to come around about Wednesday of the following week. I would continue to go back weekly for blood work. I was surprised at how much my white blood cell count had dropped, which the doctors had told me would be a normal consequence.

If the roller coaster of white blood cells, vital to my body, could ever be construed as, "normal."

I made it through my first treatment and by the third week, I was feeling myself again. But, after the second treatment, my hair began to fall out with small clumps cascading onto the shower floor and flowing into the drain.

Oh dear God, how can this be?

I decided to have my head shaved instead of watching all of my hair fall out. My neighbor came with me. Helen made me laugh through the whole process. I looked like I had signed up for the military, instead of anticipating chemo's side effects!

At the same time, I bought myself a blue baseball cap that would be my friend for the next 10 months. When my hair fell out, I knew that people would know I was a cancer patient.

Before that, I could be "normal" and no one would ever suspect I was ill. I never anticipated the amount of stares I would get with my bald head and baseball cap.

Nothing had prepared me for those responses.

It was so disconcerting the first time I went to church because I felt that everyone was staring at me as I sat during Mass, and then went up for communion.

Cancer was changing me dramatically inside and outside.

At home, I would always walk around without a hat or wig. A few times neighborhood kids came to the door and gave me that, "deer in the headlights" look, as if to say, "Hey lady, what happened to YOU!"

I would try and explain about the medicine to no avail. They were kids.

I continued to volunteer at my children's school, and participated in the PTO board, through all my chemo treatments. I was warned about being around sick kids because of the possibility of being infected, but I wanted to stay involved.

I did not want to sit home and feel sorry for myself.

I also went to the gym, even when I did not feel great. I forced myself to get up and go, and I felt such a feeling of accomplishment after I worked out.

I was winning minor skirmishes. I was NOT going to give up.

I was not going to let this disease beat me, but ...

Cancer was winning the war.

On New Year's Eve, I saw Dr. Rosen at the gym, he could not believe I was working out given I had just finished my fourth round of AC. He didn't know whether to chastise me or praise me.

I would go for my blood work and as I looked around at other patients receiving chemo I thought to myself, "*Do I look that sick?*"

I didn't feel that sick and thought I looked pretty good. It's always been hard for me to accept I had cancer because I always felt okay. I had no choice.

I was going to beat this.

I was going to live.

Cancer is vicious like that; it gives its victims false hopes.

I made it through the holidays without suffering any serious setbacks. I had a few issues with my low white blood cell count, and I came down with a bad cold, which took me off my chemo schedule for a few weeks.

At first I was disappointed, because I had mapped out all chemo treatments in three-week increments and had planned on finishing up by the end of February.

Ultimately, I completed my last round of Taxol on March

17th. "Oh my God!"

I was never so happy in my life!

My hair began growing back right after I finished the AC. My side effects with Taxol were minimal. I did lose my eyebrows and eyelashes, but I never felt sick.

There was only numbness in my hands and feet; a small price to pay for my disease.

I was just as relentless as my illness. I continued to work out and stay involved in all of my activities. I would not let cancer get me down. It would hit me and I would hit back.

I had a month off before I would start my radiation treatment.

During my chemo treatments my dear friends put together a weekly dinner schedule for our family. They prepared and served my family meals every Monday, Wednesday and Friday during chemo, and would have continued through radiation had I needed it. I was overwhelmed. My friends brought all sorts of delicious dinner meals to our home so that I would not have to cook. I was humbled.

To be so blessed to have such friends.

Their generous outpouring of support was incredible. People I didn't even know that well sent me cards and said prayers for me. I can never repay my friends and family for everything they did and continued to do for me.

I had one way to truly thank them; *by staying cancer free.*

I finally finished my last radiation treatment on June 5th. That same day I went to Arizona for a week of R & R.

I could not believe that I was finally *finished* with all the treatments.

I had very little side effects from radiation; just some redness of the skin. My arm cording came back again, and I was soon back in PT and hitting the gym again successfully bringing my arm back to its normal range of motion.

For the most part, things seemed to be looking up.

The hardest time for me came after radiation. The doctors and nurses understood my feelings and sympathized with my emotional and physical pain.

The question remained, "Where could I go now to get strong and steady emotional support?"

When you are living with cancer that is a must.

My friends and family were wonderful, but they could not truly understand what it's like to have a life-threatening illness and stare death in the face every day.

That was a battle I was fighting alone.

Granted I had a lot of support. But in the end, it was me against the cancer.

I would lie awake at night wondering if I would ever see my two boys grow up and get married. I would ask myself, "Will I be able to be a grandmother?"

And, "Will I be able to grow old with my husband?" To hold his hand and smile at his silly jokes.

Where once I took that those dreams for granted had now been placed into serious doubt.

I hated cancer.

I needed a boost for my emotional and mental struggle. I finally agreed to go on anti-anxiety medication. I felt so much better. I still worried but not as much. I'm trying not to think about recurrence. That is the fear that all of us who contract cancer dread.

I saw Dr. Tsarwhas every three months, and the days before our consultations were always filled with angst-ridden questions, "Will my blood work come back okay?" "Does the pain in my back signify cancer in my bones?"

He told me, "Joannie, what you are feeling is all very normal, and that as time goes by these feelings of anxiety will subside."

Granted, this disease was new to me. On the plus side, I've been cancer free for 14 months, and I hoped to stay that way for a long time.

My prognosis and physical strength were encouraging to me.

I was constantly trying to keep my immune system boosted to fight off any residual cancer cells. I ate as healthy as I could and exercised regularly.

I was going to beat this beast.

I continued my involvement with the PTO and school activities, and finally got my hair back. I was so happy to retire my baseball cap and my wig!

I never took days or people I loved for granted.

I appreciated life in a whole new way; the smells, the sounds, the tastes. This is such an extraordinary world we live in, and I felt blessed to have such wonderful friends and family. My two boys meant the world to me, and I pledged daily to fight so I could live to see them grow up.

I knew this had been a difficult time for them; not really understanding what cancer is as they saw me in the different phases of treatment.

Keith and I tried to be as open and honest as possible with them. They saw my surgical scars, and helped me when I did not feel that great.

Only now my older son, Andrew says, "Mom, I'm glad you have hair again."

It had really bothered him when I was bald; as much as it had bothered me. My younger son, Alex, liked to wear my wig around the house, and even wanted to use it at Halloween to decorate his pumpkin.

Now, that was funny!

I'm not going to say that I was always positive.

There were days when I wanted to lie in bed, put the covers over my head, and sleep away my fears. But, I was still a mom and I had my family to take care of and I knew I had to be strong for them and for myself.

I will keep fighting this disease and hope it does not get the better of me. I opted not to go to cancer support groups because it's too hard for me to see the pain and emotion of other cancer victims like myself.

It was too much of a constant reminder of my cancer.

I'm amazed at how much inner strength I possessed that allowed me to make it through this tumultuous year. My friends and family helped me with their support, but ultimately it was me who had to live everyday with cancer.

I have a strong spiritual base, and find myself saying many prayers, not to have a recurrence; but also for strength to get me through whatever is planned for me.

If you have cancer, I can tell you, that in the scheme of life, the treatment time is very short, and you will feel good again.

Hopefully, you will have a new appreciation for how precious life is, and to live every day to the fullest.

I did.

I just pray I can continue to experience my wonderful life for a long, long time.

~Joannie Leust

chapter sixteen

The Beauty of Hope

"We dream to give ourselves hope.
To stop dreaming – well, that's like saying
you can never change your fate."

~ Amy Tan, The Hundred Secret Senses

Hope is the driving force of the human spirit. With it, we can believe anything. Without it, we surrender everything. Nothing great was ever accomplished without hope.

Hope came into existence when man took his first breath. Great events, miracles, creative concepts and successes all had hope at their core.

Hope is the aspiration of a young actor moving to Hollywood and the foundation of every underdog in sports and the belief of anyone who ever ran for political office.

Even on Calvary, the followers of Jesus hoped for a miracle at the Resurrection. Hope has been entrenched in every human mind and every human experience.

And now, it was Joannie's strongest ally. She was hopefully optimistic that the treatments she had endured would lead her out of the storm and give her back the life she once knew.

It was a hope we all shared with her. We wanted her to be an essential part of our lives for a long time. Joannie meant the world to us.

Hope was the light that we all viewed the world in a special way.

Cancer is invisible. It moves in and around the victim's body sight unseen until it triggers a physical reaction at some point somewhere.

If the body is not behaving abnormally and the tests are not revealing any physiological irregularities, there is hope. As each day passes with no signs of cancerous activity the patient can breathe a little easier.

No news is good news.

My wife resumed her life and was thankful for each new day she woke up in the morning. She was a beautiful wife to me, loved her boys, was the glue that held both our families together and lived the way she knew how before her terrible prognosis.

She fought.

She would never give up.

She had hope.

She had faith.

It was a wonderful respite for her, especially after all the stress and pain that had defined her life as she had faced the storm.

"The very least you can do in your life is figure out what you hope for. And the most you can do is live inside that hope. Not admire it from a distance but live right in it, under its roof."

~ Barbara Kingsolver, Animal Dreams

Every hour of every day I thought about the woman I loved and was grateful for the new life she had been given. I could not even imagine my existence without her in it.

I watched her be with our two boys and I had tears of joy in my eyes as I saw how happy they were together.

I never wanted that to end.

I believed in Hope.

chapter seventeen

Devastation

*"What was more brutal than the
loss of Hope?"*

~ Nicole Mones

In March of 2004 Joannie received jolting news...

We had been spending a wonderful family vacation in San
Diego for spring break and while at the hotel we received a
phone call from her doctor.

I handed the phone to Joannie and said, "It's your doctor."

Joannie quickly reasoned that a doctor calling her on her
family vacation was bad news.

"I can't take the call, Keith." You talk to him."

She was devastated.

I nodded gently and spoke into the phone, "This is Keith, doctor. What's up?"

He went straight to the point, "Joannie's cancer is back and has spread everywhere. I'm sorry."

My body went numb. I mumbled, "Thank you," and hung up the phone. The look on my face told my wife all she needed to know. Her instincts had been correct.

"How much time do I have?" She asked me?

I shook my head, "I don't know. But, let's make the most of the time we do have, okay?"

I walked over and hugged her.

I could feel the strength fade as she held me. Her body was trembling. She began to weep and then sob uncontrollably.

I just stood there and held her.

Neither one of us said a word.

We were barely survivors on an island of Fate. And now, there was nothing we could do about it but pray and love each other the best we could.

I had never felt so empty in my entire life.

As we stood there crying together we could hear the howls of joy and laughter from our two young boys in the swimming pool a few feet away.

Our family was broken, and the boys didn't even know it.

It was a Dickensian moment; it was the best of times and the worst of times; the happiness and innocence of a child frolicking with his brother and the horrific death sentence we were now realizing together.

The look of sadness in her eyes was emotionally crippling.

In her heart she knew she had lost.

My beautiful Joannie was going to die.

Soon.

She was not going to see her two boys grow into wonderful men. She would never see them graduate from school or be part of their wedding days. She would never hold their children.

The days of her hugging and laughing with them were now numbered.

Cancer is the cruelest disease. It has no soul. It doesn't care.

I saw her heart sink. Her eyes went dead, and hope drained from her face. She sat there, ashen. Her sadness was expressed all over her face.

I could read her mind as surely as looking into a picture window of her soul, "Am I really going to die?"

"Everything that's born has to die, which means our lives are like skyscrapers. The smoke rises at different speeds, but they're all on fire, and we're all trapped."

~ Jonathan Safran Foer

I heard her whisper, "My boys."

After thinking about her limited time with them she slipped out of my arms and went to the pool. I stood at the edge of the pool as she watched them playing.

They were showing off in the water and shouting with glee.

She just kept smiling and let them know she was impressed with all their antics. It was like any normal set of moments between a mom and her children on vacation.

But, there was nothing normal here.

I saw her smile at them several times, but it was a bittersweet joy. Under her mask of seeming enjoyment lay the darker reality. She was never going to let them know it, however.

Eventually, she returned to the hotel room and I left her alone out of respect for her privacy. I stood at the door and listened to her cry. I had to brace my legs for support or I would collapse on the floor.

Soon, it would be just me and my two boys.

chapter eighteen

Spiraling Downward

"Since the day of my birth, death began its walk. It is walking toward me, without hurrying."

~ Jean Cocteau

Her Last Car

We bought Joannie a new minivan.

She unabashedly stated, "I want all the bells and whistles. This will probably be my last car and I want all the extras!"

We acceded to her wishes. It had heated seats, automatic doors and a DVD system for the boys. It even had a sun roof! She was in heaven, but every time I saw the van I couldn't help remembering her words,

"… my last car …"

I hated that phrase.

The Hour Glass

Deterioration was cancer's stranglehold on Joannie's life. She was battling each day for each breath. By the moment, her health, stamina, and spirit got steadily weaker.

Like sand flowing through an hour glass; each grain of sand was one less moment in a life that was certain to end soon.

Life was no longer full of possibilities. No longer was her death a far-off concern. My wife had a limited number of grains of sand. She had limited moments on this earth and they were flowing out very fast.

Too fast.

Living on the First Floor

In the last months of her life, Joannie was living on the first floor. She was unable to walk up the stairs to our bedroom, lacking the strength or lung capacity to walk the steps to the second floor.

She was on oxygen 24/7 as she struggled daily to breathe. I added a shower in the laundry room on the first floor, so she could bathe herself. It was a 30-foot walk from her bed to the shower. It might as well have been ten miles.

She only used it three times; she just couldn't walk that far or stand up unassisted to even wash herself. My vibrant, energetic Joannie was becoming a tragic shell of herself.

To see her struggling was beyond helpless in my spirit. I would have done anything to give her all the strength I had to see her sparkle again.

The experience of watching someone you love slowly fade way into the twilight of life at such a young age is unfathomable to healthy people.

But, it is as real as a relentless tide crushing a once virile shoreline and rendering it into a muddled mess with no form or shape. There is no more gut-wrenching than to see someone you love dissipate before your very eyes.

Her mom moved into our home allowing me to continue working so I could pay the medical bills but leaving the house each morning made me wonder if my wife would be alive when I returned that night.

How does a spouse handle that dread?

Not very well.

What / Curse

I curse this thing; this disease that
I cannot overcome

I curse it for taking the spirit
of a gifted woman

I curse this thing for taking away
our children's mother

I curse it for what it is doing to my life

I curse it, I curse it and I curse it

~ Joannie the Tigress

A physical therapist came to our house to help her regain her strength. Proudly, she would report to me as I walked through the door, "Today, I climbed three steps to the second floor, and tomorrow I will do FOUR!"

It was more than a little surreal to hear the weak voice of a woman I rarely saw physically struggling. I couldn't believe this was my Joannie.

At this point, she was two months from death.

She never again saw our bedroom on the second floor. They were unreachable heights that were just too much for her to attain.

I cried silent tears.

Divine Relief

I prayed, "If you are God, now would be a good time for you to heal her or take her home. This just doesn't seem fair to put her through all this."

False Alarm

In mid-June, 2004, Joannie's health took a profound turn for the worst. She could no longer get enough oxygen even with the full time O2 being pumped to her.

We frantically called the ambulance and rushed her to the hospital with lights and sirens blaring. Joannie laid almost lifeless on a gurney in the ambulance with me at her side.

She was terrified. I was in shock.

Really.

We were in our early forties and my wife is dying.

We were in the back of an ambulance, racing to save her life.

I could see her thoughts by the look on her face, "Was this the end?"

At the hospital they put a needle into her back penetrating her lung. She could not see what the doctor was doing. I cringed as I watched a six-inch needle inserted into her back and extracted a quart of fluid from her right lung.

Joannie had been drowning to death in her own fluids. She spent the next two weeks in the hospital, periodically having her lungs drained. One needle after another.

The cancer had spread. It was now in her lungs, in her bones and even in her brain.

It wouldn't be much longer now.

chapter nineteen
The Last Days

"Going to hospital is rather like going to an alien planet."

~ Quentin Blake

Joannie's last weeks were split between her bedroom at home and the hospital. It's funny how many times growing up you can drive by a hospital and barely notice it.

It's just a building with ambulances.

But, when you are transporting the most important person in your life to a hospital it takes on poignant significance.

Now, it is many things to you…a landmark, an edifice of impossible hope, a reminder that your life is being changed forever, a stone and mortar mixture of misery, a place you never want to be and, at the worst of times, the enemy.

There is something about entering a hospital that seems so unnatural. A human being was never meant to belong there. It only becomes necessary when the body or the mind dictates the need for your presence within its walls.

We took Joannie back and forth to the hospital. It became her way of life as much as cooking breakfast or playing with our boys.

But, it was a much darker experience than laughing in a limo or holding hands under the moon. The coldness that foreshadows the end of life is scarier than the final breath. It is a hopeless exercise of dread that must be carried out from the waiting lobby to the pained look on a doctor's face as he delivers the horrific news.

That is a hospital.

A place that was to save those with the most horrific illnesses.

The Vigil

In the hospital Joannie was never alone.

I would not allow it. She was my precious. No matter what, she would be taken care of by those who loved her. She would NEVER be alone. She would NEVER wake up wondering. She would NEVER feel pain without someone holding her hand.

While the staff was competent, the state of medical care just doesn't provide the constant coverage needed to always ensure the patient's potential emergencies.

As a result, I decided that as a family one of us would be with her constantly.

She would never be alone.

Never wake up wondering "… where am I" "What is going on."

I was determined that she would always wake up to a smiling face from someone she knew and loved to give her the comfort and reassurance that she deserved.

We did shifts.

We were fortunate. We had a large family. The Lehman's, the consummate 'lovers of life' were at Joannie's side. My family, did their part, provide an anchor in the storm for the boys. A safe and loving place of stability.

A family member was in the hospital room constantly. Someone would always spend the night by her side. We were there to watch soap operas and Judge Judy during the day.

I would never want to be married to Judge Judy, by the way. She scares me!

Big Al

I was still working, but on a reduced schedule. Each morning Joannie's dad and I would go to the hospital to relieve whoever spent the night.

During that fifteen-minute ride we talked about Joannie. He held onto his faith and prayed for a miracle. It is very difficult to see a father lose his child.

He was heartbroken.

His prayers were answered but not in the way he wanted. She left this Earth knowing she would never see her children grow up.

Big Al had a huge heart that broke a little more each day. He had always hoped there would be a miracle and that she would get better, but as he saw his daughter wasting away his hope slowly faded with her.

The man who loved to laugh began to cry.

The Sisters

Sometimes, Joannie's sisters accompanied me to her room. I would greet Joannie with a smile and tell her how much better she looked than the day before. Her sisters looked askance at me. We all knew I was telling lies for Joannie's sake.

It was always a non-negotiable aspect of our visit with her.

This Little Piggy

There is a game that most parents have played with their young children. You gently tug on each toe, starting with the big toe. Saying "this little piggy went to market …," well we all know the rhyme.

At the end you run your fingers up their leg and tickle them under the chin!

I did this to Joannie as she lied in her hospital bed. It created an incredible connection between us.

She smiled every time I did this. It reminded both of us of times when things were happy, safe and the future was bright.

In this simple act, we both remembered when our children were just babies; times which were so incredibly happy. The giggles of our boys when we played "*This Little Piggy*" with them would send chills down our spines.

They were so happy.

It connected us in a way that only a husband and wife, a father and mother could appreciate.

By doing this to Joannie, she would wait expectantly for my fingers to run up her side and tickle her under her chin. She cooed and smiled, and the room lit up for an instant.

And, for a moment we both shared a flicker of a past happiness.

We were always connected, and this simple act made her smile. She was safe, if only for a minute.

Andrew and Alex

I brought the boys to visit their mom several times in the hospital each week in the evening. It was tough on them to see their mom so vulnerable, but Joannie ached to be with them. She needed to hold their hands and look into their eyes.

She was their mom until her dying breath.

Celebrating Alex's Birthday

We gave our youngest son a party in the intensive care ward of the hospital. He turned eight years old that day. We substituted plastic forks for lit birthday candles because of all the oxygen in the environment to prevent the room from blowing up and killing us all.

Wouldn't that have been ironic!

The "Wolf" and the End

On a quiet afternoon I found myself in a "family waiting room" in the hospital my wife was admitted to. I was sitting with my wife's oncologist discussing the last-ditch efforts that were being taken to treat my wife's breast cancer.

As we talked, it became clear that all options had been exhausted and that my wife would soon die. As this reality slowly sank into me, I became aware of a deep wailing coming from somewhere nearby.

It sounded like the cry of a lone wolf in deep mortal pain. It was haunting sound with the ghoulish depths of emotion of pain.

It was frightening.

I had never heard anything so mournful, so unsettling in my life. I looked around the lobby to see who was in such agony, wondering what they could be feeling which was clearly breaking their spirit.

At first, I thought the sound was coming from a nearby waiting room. But, as I paused and listened, I realized that the cries were coming from deep within me.

I was the one wailing, crying out in a pain that began deep within my soul. I was shocked to realize how overwhelmed I was by the depth of it all.

At that moment nothing existed, all I felt was my heart breaking. There was no thought of the past or the future.

I was awash in searing sorrow.

My spirit was broken. There was nothing left.

Hope. Prayer. Belief. It was all gone.

Joannie was going to die, no matter what or how we offered ourselves up to the heavens above.

There was no hope. I was going to have to tell my Joannie that all hope was gone.

I was going to have to tell our children that their mother was going to die.

The finality broke my heart. It broke spirit. It took my soul.

God left me with nothing.

What I Fear

A poem written late one night as I struggled with our reality.

I loathe the still and the quiet
I fear the night, for it brings out the memories of the past and the uncertainties of the future
The silent sobbing of helplessness
The fear of what the morning will bring

I loathe the pain of a wife fighting a silent dread eating away at her body
I desperately seek for strength to keep her from dropping into despair
I struggle with the constant pain that she endures so that she can bear witness to her children's life

I hate the helplessness I feel each night, as I try to comfort a young son struggling with the realities of life
I struggle to find meaning in an existence so full of pain and uncertainty
Yet I love the laughter of my boy as they delight in tickles and hugs
The innocence of youth

I fear for my own mortality and my obligation to educate my children to the ways of life
The inevitable pain and sorrow, the love and the joy that awaits them
I gasp with the knowledge that I cannot protect my children from what lies ahead
Knowing that they too risk experiencing the cruelty of life

I am lost in the loneliness of the dark
Wandering, listening and praying for hope, finding only darkness
Forsaken by what so many call God
Each night I look around and find that I am alone, listening to the sobs of my dying wife
I need solace, I pray for a respite

I am forlorn, knowing that at the end of each day,
I will once again face myself, alone
Relentlessly the days are coming, days in which
I will lose all that is precious
The love of my life will be stripped away
My anchors of strength, the threads of hope will all fade

Each night I shed tears of self-pity, wishing it were not so
I lay awake, drifting silently
Listening to the soft breath of my dying wife
Waiting for sleep to come and rescue me from this harsh reality

- December 9, 2003

Noah's Ark Visitation

Joannie's friends came in twos to visit her. Her sister Sharon presided over the visitation. It lifted her spirits and three people made it more festive than two. It also gave her friends to lean on each other when they saw my sweet wife suffering.

Sharon oversaw the process. In the few years we were in Illinois Joannie had become tightly connected to a special group of moms.

Each in their own way feared their own loss of being a mother. Each were tightly connected to Joannie as a member of a special sorority; women that would raise their children to be unique.

Unique in that they would always be loved by their mother.

Ten pairs of women visited Joannie on the third day before her death. Each pair had but 45 minutes to say hello and a final goodbye.

I don't know what was said, but I am certain that it contained the promise to watch over our boys.

To this day I struggle to appreciate how difficult those last conversations were with my Joannie and her closest friends.

To realize that she was about to die and knowing how much she hoped that others would follow through on their promise to watch over her children but never knowing if it would be so, must have been agony for her.

It must have taken all the faith she had to trust me and others who would fulfill her last wish.

A Fiesta North of the Border!

During Joannie's last stay in the hospital she mentioned in passing to our Irish neighbor, "I think it would be fun to have a Margarita party in the hospital!"

That was all she needed to say.

Helen gave Joannie a gift that outshone anything we could have imagined. She gave Joannie smiles, laughter and for a few hours an escape from the battle being fought. To this day the memory of Helen's gift brings smiles. Cheers!

The following day we had 30 people in her hospital room drinking margaritas and eating salsa with tortilla chips that our neighbor had mischievously snuck into the hospital.

One of the nurses came in just as the festivities began and saw the cocktail in Joannie's hand. She pulled me aside and told me, "Mr. Leust, it is totally inappropriate for your wife to be drinking alcohol in her condition. She is a very sick woman!"

I shot back, "She is also a dying woman, and this is her last request. A drink is certainly not going to change her physical condition at this point. I appreciate your concern; now I hope for your understanding. We want her to be happy. It's the least we can do for her now."

With that I handed her a margarita. It was all I could do.

The nurse nodded and gave me a faint smile and exited the room. Nurses are as savvy and professional as they come.

When word began to leak to the nurse's station that we were

having a Margarita party we were swarmed by the other RN's who came in to observe this happy therapy: A cocktail party in the cancer ward!

These professional men and women understood we were celebrating Joannie's life and this was a wonderfully appropriate way to do it.

As the Margaritas splashed on the linoleum floor it got on the soles of everyone's shoes and we all found ourselves laughing to the sticky sound of sneakers up and down the hall. We had left lasting tracks in the cancer ward that day.

Ole'

Surrounded by Family

Near the end we crowded around her one last time. A priest arrived in her room and played the dulcimer, plucking the strings in musical harmony.

We wanted to honor her with the sights and sounds of those she loved. Her smile told us all that she felt special.

A fact we always knew about her.

Post-hospital Care

Joannie was to be discharged from the hospital as there was nothing else they could do for her. The staff gave me a list of local assisted living places for me to visit.

Their thinking was that she would need constant care and

that such a facility could provide it.

I went with Joannie's sister, Mary, to visit several places. We only checked out two facilities. I am sure that they would have provided great care, but they had that stale smell of death.

I am sorry, my wife was not going to die there.

It was now clear to me that Joannie would never be alone, that she would be at home where the family and I could provide the care she needed, not just physically, but emotionally and spiritually.

We lived one day at a time knowing that the inescapable truth of life followed by death would occur and praying that it wouldn't be today.

A Letter to Andrew and Alex

I asked Joannie to write a letter to our boys. Something they could read when they reached 18 years-old.

She just couldn't do it.

It would be an admission that she was going to die and not be there for their 18th birthday. It was something she could not accept. Later, she asked if I would get a video camera so that she could *record* a message for to them.

I bought a video camera and told her that whenever she was ready we could prepare her personal message to them.

She never asked. I never pushed.

Wingman Walt

John (Walt), Joannie's brother, became my wingman for the last two weeks of her life. He and his girlfriend Stephanie took off time from their lives, and moved into our home. He gave me the Hospice Book, "*Crossing the Creek*," by Michael Holmes, during her last hours which really touched me.

John was there as a man for me to talk to, to listen to me, to acknowledge the pain that I was going through.

He was an anchor in the storm.

I will be forever grateful to him.

John, thank you. You helped me stand tall, and walk a path that no husband, no father ever imagined having to walk.

The Family of Fun

The Lehman's and my mother joined us a week before she died.

All four of her sisters and her two brothers arrived and Joannie lit up like the Aurora Borealis!

They spent time in the house with Joannie, telling stories, laughing and remembering their lives together.

To see her so happy meant the world to me.

She passed away three days later.

The struggle was over.

Joannie battled cancer for almost two years.

Suddenly it was over.

Done. The finality was overwhelming.

Why Me?

I will never forget Joannie imploring me, "Why me, Keith? Why do I have to die?"

Her big brown eyes pleaded with me for an answer.

The tears slowly flowed down her cheeks.

"Keith, …I don't want to die. I don't want to leave the boys and you behind."

'Please help me. I beg you, don't let me die'

She was crying intensely now, "Why me?" I have been good. I trusted God to take care of me. I trusted that I would be able to see my children grown up. I trusted that I would not bestow such pain on them."

I was helpless. Watching my wife; the mother of our children, being eaten away by the incessant devastation of cancer was impossible to fathom. There was no relief.

Joannie sobbed to me through her tears, "Will I be okay?"

What could I say; the surgery had confirmed the worst. I confidently smiled and stated, "Yes, you are going to be fine!"

It was a lie of love.

There was only the grim truth, she would soon die. There was, and still is, no answer.

Breaking the News

After discussing the plan with Father Fred, our parish priest, I explained to Joannie she needed to sit down with Andrew and Alex and gently say goodbye to them.

She refused.

"I'm their mom; I'm not going to tell them I am going to die. That will be too hurtful for all of us. I don't want to see their hearts broken here. You are my husband and their father, Keith. It is your role to talk to our sons."

I nodded, "Okay, honey. I am sorry for upsetting you. I'll take care of it."

I hugged her and felt her sobbing into my chest. That night I sat down with Andrew and Alex and gently talked to them.

I started off telling them, "Mommy is very sick and that she is not going to get better."

I waited a moment for that to sink in. They were eight and nine years old. Just kids.

Then I added, "Because mommy is so sick she is going to die soon."

Immediately they both asked me, "How soon?"

I choked up and rasped, "Within a few weeks."

Andrew stood up and began walking randomly around the room. He was emotionally lost. His lack of experience had no way to process this horrific piece of information.

I just let him process his grief as he paced in circles.

Alex climbed up on my lap and stared at me with his deep, soulful eyes. He just huddled against me. I was too choked up to say anything, too.

Finally he stated, "Dad, things will never be the same."

I could only agree with him, so profound was his statement.

We spent about an hour together, Alex sobbing and Andrew not at all accepting the news. I assured them that I would always be here for them and that I was healthy and not going anywhere.

We then went to their mother's room and had the conversation again. I did the talking, Joannie sobbed and silently agreed with what I was saying.

There was nothing else to say. She was going to die, and things would never be the same.

The next day, the boys fed their mom berries and kept hugging her. Nothing was said about her fate but there were tears, physical gestures and a lot of berries being shared.

Andrew and Alex went from being her sons to being her caregivers. They let go of her role as their mother and nurtured her. Feeding her the sweet tenderness that only a berry can give another person.

The roles had been *reversed*.

I have never been so proud of them.

The Last Drive Home

We left the hospital so my beautiful Joannie could die at home. I will always have the memory of the raindrops on her face as we walked to the ambulance. She smiled as we rolled the gurney to the front door. Light rain drops falling on her face. It was the first time in several weeks that she was outside. The sky's seemed to be crying, as I hid my own tears.

They were mixed with the real tears.

The following night we invited Mark, the priest, to our home where he played his dulcimer for all of us.

Over two dozen people were packed into the family room including, Joannie's family, my mother and a few of her dearest friends celebrating her life.

She smiled from her bed, basking in the love that surrounded her.

It wasn't the Beatles on Ed Sullivan but it was pretty sweet music to us!

Of Course, The Funeral Home

My friend from college, a brother that I never had, Heinzy and I made plans for Joannie's death. I felt like Brutus preying on Caesar; the ultimate betrayal.

But, arrangements had to be made. We visited the funeral home and we were ushered into a room filled with urns.

As I held the various urns the thought that one of these would be holding the ashes of the woman I had loved as my wife sent a surreal chill through me.

I remember thinking, "This isn't happening; my Joannie will never be inside one of these. She is too alive and vibrant to even imagine this."

In the end, I picked one out. Heinzy and I made our way into the sunlight back to the car.

I was as numb as I had ever been. It had been a sobering morning with an emotionally devastating reality that the end was near.

Now, I was holding a life after death urn.

Dear Lord, give me strength.

I have betrayed my wife. I am planning her death.

A Woman's Best Friend

As I was keeping vigil over Joannie at home in the final hours, our dog, Tasha, suddenly leaped into her bed to say goodbye. Joannie's spirit was slowly fading, and Tasha seemed to know. She was not to be denied. She would pay her last respects. She would say goodbye to our Joannie.

As I watched her snuggle up against her, I fought to hold back tears.

Pretty special.

Shutting Down

As the minutes ticked away, I felt Joannie's legs and arms as they became cold to the touch. Her legs were also numb and filled with fluids causing them to be swollen.

She couldn't move her limbs.

She unsuccessfully tried to rise up and look at her legs. She murmured, "I feel so ugly."

'Please don't let me go.'

I smiled warmly at her, "No, you look absolutely beautiful."

She settled back on her pillow with an ashen color to her face and smiled weakly at me. I thought to myself, "So, this is what dying is like."

chapter twenty

One Last Kiss

"We both know it's better if we just let it go. So, let's have one last kiss, one last touch, one last tender moment between us."

~ Bino

I will never forget our final time together. It was at night. Somehow the night brings a different feeling to who we are.

There had been countless nights that I had simply held my wife as she slowly fell asleep.

She needed to be held long after she had slipped into the depths of her sleep. She needed to know that she was not alone. That I was there to help protect her against the unknown.

As I held her in those moments she would murmur her most intimate fears to me, "Please don't let me go. Don't let me die."

All I could do was to gently run my hand over her back, caress her and whisper, "Shh, everything is going to be okay." "I have got you."

It was a lie that needed to be said. It tore me up to say it but it was even more devastating to realize the truth of it.

As she drifted deeper to sleep, her body would twitch, almost as if she was fighting off demons of death that were clawing for her.

I held her tighter, assuring her, "Joannie, I am right here next to you. I am always here. I will never leave you, honey."

That last statement was only partially true. She would be leaving me. Saying goodbye is like that. You say things that the dying person needs to hear because they beg to be comforted and you ache to comfort them.

In those moments I was holding her all that mattered was that I loved her and that I was doing everything I could to maintain her sense of safety and keep her hopes up for the future Joannie wanted for us and our two boys.

With each passing week, this became more difficult for me. She was becoming increasingly frailer yet she yearned for my touch. My presence at her side, the security, the strength, the promise that all would be okay.

I found myself lying awake long into the night, gently stroking her hair, touching her cheek and always whispering into her ear that I loved her, that I would always be there taking care of her and our boys.

Ever more gently as each touch triggered her cancer-infused

nerves to jump, I needed to find a way around her discomfort and fear. It took all the emotional and mental strength I had to always be there for her.

Dying is not subtle; nor is it for the faint of heart.

To hold the woman that you loved, as she slowly fell under the spell of sleep was a gift. She trusted me that I was always there to protect her.

She was at her most vulnerable place in her life.

Ever.

Joannie just wanted to be cared for. She wanted to be treated like a princess. She wants you to be with her. To share her dreams. To be her partner through whatever darkness that she is experiencing and that we do not understand.

To help her through the pain of chemo, the sorrow of letting go, the horror of leaving her young children behind.

I learned that the best I could give. The most that I could love. The only thing that mattered was to hold her. To tenderly whisper to her. To stroke her hair. To caress her forehead. To tuck the blanket carefully around her. To give her my heart and pray that it would be enough.

I strived to stay awake. To feel what each movement, each twitch and what each murmur required. Minutes in the dark feel like hours, in fact they can feel like forever.

I wanted to keep her alive. To experience each precious breath.

I needed to be there for her. To be the anchor, the light that made it ok to succumb to the depths of sleep. The depths of darkness that might hold unimagined terrors that reflected the reality of being awake.

So, I lay with my wife. Barely six inches from her face. Listening to her breath. Holding her hand. Knowing that she is asleep. Listening to each breath. Feeling each twitch. Responding in kind. Whispering in her ear. Telling her that all is 'ok'.

Gently hugging her close so that she can feel my heart beat, knowing that she is alive.

Stillness

One moment there is life; in the blink of an eye, there is death. It reminded me of a poignant quote,

Life asked death, "Why do people love me but hate you?" Death responded, "Because you are a beautiful lie and I am a painful truth."

And, in the stillness of that moment, that truth was about to become Joannie's reality.

For twenty years since I had first met her I knew it was time to forever let her go. It wasn't done with fanfare or fireworks; it was a quiet admission in a quiet room where nothing could be heard and nothing was said.

Only stillness.

One Last Kiss

All of the family, the Leust's and the Lehman's were there when she exhaled her last breath. As soon as I heard it, I leaned down and briefly touched my lips to hers.

I didn't want her to leave without it.

Joannie died on July 11, 2004 at 7:50 p.m. just as the sun was beginning to set.

Fitting.

chapter twenty-one
Joannie Says Goodbye

The Star

We all felt Joannie's spirit slip from her body, it hovered in the room for a moment and silently dissipated.

Then there was a loud sobbing and crying which emanated from all of us. Andrew ran out of the family room onto the deck, and back into the kitchen on the other side.

My mother was watching him and ran to him, holding him.

My son was terrified. He kept blubbering, "I can't breathe!"

His anguish could not be consoled, he did not cry; he was numb with pain. My mother brought Andrew to me but I also could not take the pain away.

I just kept holding my shaking boy tightly in my arms.

To get sons away from this pain in the room, my mother took them outside to the front of the house. It was getting dusk but no stars could yet be seen. She told them to look for a star in the sky because that will be Mom waving to them and that she would be there every evening for them.

Everyone then also followed them out as devastated warriors had trusted Spartacus and looked to him for a sign of hope. Within moments, we were all standing on the front lawn, guided by a young boy's gaze as he looked up excitedly for the first twinkle of light in the evening sky.

The light Alex believed was his mother's soul was being born as a star. We waited anxiously for him to find it, for we instinctively knew that he would discover it and show us his mother.

The new star in God's heaven.

The wait was breathless as our eyes searched everywhere for a new ray of night light above us. It was set up by the setting sun, with its glorious colors that had not been seen all summer, lighting up the horizon.

Then high clouds blanketed the heavens. As my little boy focused on his visual mission we all looked at each other as if to ask, "Were there no new stars being born tonight?"

Then suddenly Alex spotted the Star!

He excitedly exclaimed, "There is Mommy, she is right there!"

Our hearts danced.

Joannie was still alive in Alex's heart, as sure and strong as if she were physically standing beside him. We all felt the wonder in the sky and hoped that it was Joannie twinkling to us.

Andrew looked on, knowing that his mother was gone, but now believing that he had a guardian angel watching over him. He also understood that a guardian angel was no substitute for his mother's love on earth but, it was something.

It was enough for him at that moment.

The Funeral

I arrived at St. Anne's church for Joannie's visitation and funeral not knowing what to expect. The loss of the most important person in my life had left me in raw emotional territory.

Upon arriving I realized that no one from the family had yet entered the visitation room. They were all standing outside, heads bowed solemnly. I was expected to enter first.

I couldn't do it and told Big Al as much.

He was also struggling to enter the room. This was his daughter. The one that helped keep the family together. The woman whose spirit brought life into everything the family did together.

Finally, he put his hand on the middle of my back, and gently guided me into the room, where we stood together looking at my wife and his daughter.

She looked like an angel finally at peace.

All the pain and suffering was gone. She had a serenity about her. The battle that had waged in her body for two long years had ended her life but in the end, Joannie's spirit had emerged victorious.

Joannie believed in Easter and the resurrection of Jesus. She was experiencing it now in the glorious end of her earthly life just as he had.

"O death, where is your victory?
O death, where is your sting?"

~1 Corinthians 15:55

The peaceful expression on her face told me that she was in an eternal place and not alone.

That was comforting to me.

There was a two-hour visitation to anyone who wished to pay their last respects. Slowly, one by one people began to arrive and then the floodgates of grieving people arrived to pay their respects for the Joannie they loved.

There were scores of people, all waiting quietly to enter the visitation room. I found myself at the doorway, standing and greeting people, thanking them for their kind words and their presence.

I flashed back to our wedding where I had stood next to her in the reception line as we greeted all our guests, Joannie and I thanking them for participating in our marriage.

Only now I was standing alone, thanking them as we said goodbye to her.

My bride was no longer at my side.

I would have given anything to hold her hand like we had done in a happier time.

Now, I knew what to expect at her memorial service.

The finality of her earthly presence was officially gone.

I would never hold her hand again.

The hours passed in moments with the same conversation over and over again from so many wonderful people, who possessed such sorrow in their hearts, for Joannie, for me and the boys and our families.

At the end, I was completely *exhausted*. Holding this memorial service together was like Atlas carrying the weight of the world upon his shoulders.

At that point, the priest called everyone back into the church for the final ceremony. I was left standing alone, with Joannie's body in the visitation room.

I could not leave her side.

I knew that once I left the visitation room her casket would be closed, and I would never see her again. I stood there, alone at her side, weeping.

I had been with Joannie for 20 years, and now I was expected to simply let her go. To relinquish two decades of building a family together.

I felt as if I was about to collapse into the floor, the pain of my loss was pulling me into the depths of an abyss.

Just then Annette, my dear sister, walked into the room.

She took me into her arms and held me and made the pain ours; not just mine. She carried my soul up from the depths of darkness and gave me comfort at a moment when I thought I would never be able to survive the loss.

Thank you, my dear sister. I can never fully express how much you meant to me on that day.

In that moment.

Annette got me out of that room and walked me back into the church. I was humbled by the number of people that stood reverently as I struggled to walk to where our family stood.

As Annette tried to help me, my mother went to the boys to be with them because they also were asked to leave the room.

The Mass began and ended with the same grace that Joannie had lived her life. Everyone struggled with the awareness that she was no longer part of our existence.

She had a new life now. A forever existence.

Dramatically, after Joannie's sisters and brothers had stood and expressed their eulogies, a bright stream of sun light broke through the atrium at the top of the church and illuminated the entire hall.

Joannie was saying goodbye.

With her warm smile we all knew and loved.

Responding to Their Mother's Death

Andrew and Alex expressed their grief in different ways at the end of Joannie's final moments on earth. My oldest son, taking after his dad, internalizes everything. He needs time to get away and process the serious moments in his life.

Later that evening, Annette, Astrid and my mother took the boys and cousins downstairs to talk about their mom, and play games with them to try to lessen their pain temporarily.

Both boys did not sleep alone that night. My sisters and my mother stayed for several days and lightened and brightened the days as best they could.

Annette visited us the following summer for several weeks with Rebecca and Ryan, her children. It was a time when my boys, particularly Andrew, really bonded with her. She is a most caring and loving mother, a fun-filled and insightful person.

To this day, Annette and Andrew are very close. My sister told me that one time Andrew had almost called her, "mom." Annette choked up with tears when she related that moment to me.

She was relieved he didn't use that word in addressing her. Andrew was reliving his love for his mother through my sister.

Understandable.

Andrew had a mom. She would always be there and love him and Alex. After all, they were 'my precious boys'. With that there is a smile that cannot ever be diminished.

Her name is Joannie Leust.

Forever.

Alex spent his grieving time as a philosopher, blurting out insight after insight as his way of exhaling his pain.

With time he recognized the brightness of life, and felt his mother's pride in how he would embrace life. One experience after another.

Beyond the Sea

Big Al and Carrie accompanied me and my boys to the ocean in Florida. It was time for scattering Joannie's ashes into the sea. After all this was Joannie's wish, to be made part of the ocean. Part of the world. She didn't want us hovering around a cold burial plot in years to come.

It wasn't quite what I had expected.

As I reached into the urn and pulled out a handful of ashes I felt pieces of grit mixed in with them. They were tiny bone fragments of the woman I loved.

I was stunned and appalled at the sensation they caused in my hand.

The ashes were benign, gentle and unassuming.

But, the bone fragments were a chilling reminder that I was truly holding the remains of the woman I had loved and it jarred my senses as I realized she was once a living human being.

That was a heartbreaker for me.

I shut down emotionally to survive the moment and tossed her ashes into the air.

As we stood there and watched them fly skyward. They reminded us of Joannie herself…the ashes magically swirling around our boys, Alex and Andrew. They seemed like tiny fireflies in the twilight.

As they settled on them. It was like their mother was touching them one last time; comforting them and saying goodbye (maybe she was saying "hello"). They looked at their shoulders and smiled.

Mom was right there.

The Visitor

My youngest sister, Astrid, shared some stunning revelations with me in the days following Joannie's death.

Here are her exact words,

> *"The night Joannie died I laid on the bed in the kitchen/family room in which she had passed away. She lay on my chest and could feel her arms like angel wings wrapping around me.*
>
> *I shared the bed with Alex that night on which she passed*

away and I felt her come into the room and I sensed her telling me, "Please reach out and touch my son."

I suddenly realized she wanted me to touch Alex so she could touch him. She did so and even though that little boy was asleep. I heard him murmur,

'Mommy.'

It was a glorious experience to be part of Joannie's final good-bye. Much later, when the two boys were older and sitting with me in St. Patrick's Cathedral in New York City, I told them about their mother coming to me.

On another occasion, as I was piling Joannie's boys and my children into the mini-van for a trip to the grocery store, my two year-old daughter blurted out, "Aunt Joannie is here. I felt her."

I believe she felt Joannie's spirit with them that moment.

Once a mom; always a mom.

To this day, Alex is metaphysically spiritual, perhaps, because he wishes to see and touch her again.

chapter twenty-two
Moving Forward

"You must let the pain visit.
You must allow it teach you.
You must not allow it overstay."

~ Ijeoma Umebinyuo

I have moved on. But I still hang on to the past. To what might have been.

To what was lost.

Yet my life continues.

I had two precious boys to take care of now. Two boys to love and raise without a mom teaching them how to become healthy and loving men.

It is what Joannie wanted me to do. It is what we wanted to

do together.

This journey has been gritty, grinding and grievously painful. It has been an ordeal that has brought such personal and all-encompassing sadness to every part of my being.

Every step of the way has gradually cut deeply into my spirit.

One by one, the details of her horrendous disease had slashed my hope. It was a torturous death march...The news that my wife had cancer...the reality that her life would be cut short...the realization that our children would grow up without her...the horror of knowing that in the months ahead...and eventually, the fact that we would all become aware that she would have tremendous pain waiting for her.

And the final *result*?

There would be an end; and it would be the most fatal step of all.

My wife died too soon, in an overwhelming way.

She was bullied by a disease that toyed with her emotions, mocked her false hopes and finally smashed her spirit and body to dust.

It was too hard to bear.

Now, I will make sense of it and have hope again.

My inspiration in moving ahead came from Joannie herself. I remembered how proud she had been when she was able to walk up three steps; believing that the harder she tried, the better her chances would be.

She never gave up. I can hear her voice in my head even now,

"Keith, Never Give Up!"

As painful her struggle, she always tried to keep moving forward. She adamantly refused to give in to her disease, always believing she would overcome her cancer.

If she could do that before she died; I will do that after she died.

Thank you, my beautiful Joannie.

Who Matters

Years ago, a dear friend Myra shared a lesson that I have never forgotten.

As you go through life you will become acquaintances with 'friends of the road', and if you are lucky you will also become connected with those who will always be 'friends of the heart'.

'Friends of the road' are those people that you have a relationship with for the time that you are together. Be it as school friends, work colleagues, or even neighbors. You are friends because you have something in common.

Then there are 'friends of the heart'. Individuals that you connect on a much deeper level. These are people that you share common values, beliefs, and see the world in the same kind of way. You are connected because you value life, family, friends and those around you in similar ways.

'Friends of the road' are great. They help you navigate the day to day. 'Friends of the heart' are those who are there when you need someone to listen to your deepest thoughts, hopes, pain and joy. They are the people that you can count on, no matter what.

When Joannie died we had lived in the Midwest for just four years. We arrived here with no friends or family. We knew no one.

At Joannie's funeral there were over 300 individuals. People who mourned the loss of a 'friend of the heart'.

To this day, I am honored to have known and been part of Joannie's life. A woman that made a difference in so many lives.

Who Should Care for the Boys

After Joannie died both my sisters-in-law and my own sisters offered to help raise my boys. It turned out that this was not an offer or a suggestion, but rather a judgement. I was deemed to be a broken man, not well equipped to raise to young boys. The collective thinking was that my boys, Andrew and Alex, needed more than a dad that was grieving.

A man who clearly was just a shell of his former self.

The boys needed much more that their dad could offer.

So, a decision was made by the well-intentioned women in

our life that the boys should be raised by someone other than Keith.

I recognized this as both their way of helping 'take care' of my boys as well as absolving me of the responsibility of raising children on my own.

I was at a cross roads.

How to appreciate that fact that these wonderful women wanted to take the responsibility of raising children that were not their own. To ensure that the boys would receive the love, attention and stability that they thought they would provide.

Yet, it was incredibly insulting.

These were MY boys. Andrew and Alex were now my children. My responsibility. As a family Joannie and I were committed to doing everything, … anything to raising the boys as best as we could.

With Joannie gone, nothing changed. I was responsible, accountable and honored to be the boy's dad.

Their parent.

I was going to raise them. I was going to do exactly what Joannie and I agreed to do. While she was not physically here, I was going to be their parent and provide them with the very best that I could.

I was not going to ship the boys off to someone else to raise. Memories of my dad being sent to an orphanage because his dad simply could not take care of his children were flashed in front of me.

I was going to raise our children.

Joannie and I wanted children together. I was determined to be our boys parent and raise them well.

The sisters relented, recognizing that I was not going to give up my boys. I had my conviction and Joannie's strength.

I would raise our children, and do a great job doing it. Nothing else mattered for me.

HELP!

While I was determined to raise the boys, I also recognized that the boys and I were broken. Nothing prepared us to lose their mom, my wife.

This is uncharted territory. Family, friends, colleagues were quick to offer advice, suggestions, ideas on how to move forward. But none of them had any real experience in what we were living.

I found a wonderful child psychologist. Dr. Michelle. She became the outlet, sounding board, anchor for both the boys and me. For over three years we met with her several times a month.

First, I met with her to provide an update as to what was going on, and then she met with Andrew and Alex separately to listen, empathize and provide coping tools to help get them through the next few days.

They slept in my room, together on a separate bed, so that I was always close to them. They needed to be close to me. Close to one another.

The darkness of each night reinforced their fear that somehow we might be separated, was calmed by the three of us being in the same room.

It took a year before the boys could sleep in their own bedrooms.

Small steps.

Dad Will You Die Too?

We live in a neighborhood that is really great to walk in. Each evening the boys and I would walk what we called the rainbow walk. We called it the 'rain bow' walk because years earlier when their mom was alive we walked the same path after a thunder storm only to see a remarkable rainbow.

Fourteen years later we still called it the rainbow walk.

Several weeks after their mom died, the boys and I took our evening walk. As we walked Andrew reached out and held my hand. "Dad are you going to die too?"

As a single parent how do you answer this?

I could promise him and his brother that I would always be there for them. But what if a car came around the curve at that very moment and killed me. I would have lied to them. Broken my promise to be there for them as they grieved for the loss of their mom.

In that moment I realized how fragile the boys were. How fragile my family was.

They were counting on me. Desperately hoping that they would not lose their last hold on stability. A foundation that as children, they counted on. Their parents.

Their mom was dead. They watched her die. They saw their mom in a coffin. They said goodbye.

They could not afford to lose their dad too.

I paused and said the best that I could.

"Boys I will do the very best that I can and always try to be here for you."

"I love you both dearly and will do everything I can to be here for you."

We are all fortunate.

Their dad is still alive.

Today they are grown men, each with their own independent life. A job, apartment, a healthy relationship. We speak several times every week. They will always be my boys. I will always be their dad.

They are now self-reliant recognizing the fragility of life. Happy to be part of our family and at the same time looking forward to creating their own future. A future creating their own family.

The Family is Broken

There are hidden groups that we never see. After Joannie died several men reached out to me. Men who also lost their wives. Each with their own story of pain and tragedy. Some with children that they were now raising by themselves, others who never had the opportunity to start a family and were now alone.

I never appreciated that there were others who experienced and suffered as I had. Mostly silent. Suffering and enduring that only men can do.

Through them I came to fully appreciate that my family was broken. Joannie, my wife, the boy's mom was gone.

We were once a family of four. Dad, mom and the two boys.

That was broken and no longer existed. It could not be healed. Not fixed. Ever.

I had to accept that I now had a new family.

Me and my boys, ... without Joannie. Without their mom. Without my wife.

Dead Wife's Club

It is interesting how like finds like. After Joannie died I came to know other men who were also widowers. Men whose wives had died.

A grim club. But only we could understand one another.

There was no "… I can imagine what you are going through." No, these fellow travelers experienced exactly what I was going through. There was an unspoken understanding. We know one another's pain.

In this understanding we helped one another.

One dad, a widower, shared with me how he had to rethink his family.

"Keith, before your wife died you had a family of four. You, Joannie and your two boys. Nothing was more important than the circle that surrounded the four of you."

"Now that your wife is gone, you have to remake your family. It is now a family of three. You, and your two boys. Establish this as the new normal. Embrace it. Take care of your new family. There is no room for deep grief when you are raising your children."

Strong words to live by.

A New Normal

Living as a family of three was difficult. I had to become both the dad and the mom. The one to provide the discipline and at the same time the one to give the hugs and murmurs of 'everything will be ok'.

A difficult balance. How to provide the male, masculine boundaries that boys need while still giving the hugs and kisses when they fall and scrape their knee. When they are bullied at school or when they don't do as well as they hoped on that math test.

Being a Mom / Dad sucks.

There were times I resented Joannie being dead. Leaving me behind to take care of everything. We promised each other that we would create and raise a family together.

I upheld my end.

I am alive. I was taking care of our family.

Where was she?

No, I am not angry with Joannie. She fought hard. She did not die without a fierce fight. She would not leave her boys behind. She fought like a lion against the injustice of cancer. Fighting for each inch. For each minute to be alive so that she could be with our boys.

Each minute. Every second was precious.

And she lost.

I am honored to be left behind to raise and take care of our boys. They are our treasure.

Time does NOT heal all wounds. But time does allow us to move on (if we are ready). To be strong. To persevere. To take care of what is most important, ... our family.

Breathing Deeply

I have always known that being married to a remarkable woman would be a gift. To share my life with someone who shares my values, beliefs and hopes would make my life extraordinary.

It took me into my mid-twenties to realize this.

Yes, I am a stupid man. It took me too long to realize how much fuller my life would be with a remarkable woman.

With this realization, I did not want to be alone.

I did not want the boys to grow up without a female influence as part of their life.

There was never a plan to replace their mother, rather I sought to add a vital part to our family that was missing.

A woman who would love each of us unconditionally.

A woman who could help me be a better mom / dad.

A woman that I would find love with and cherish.

A woman that the boys would look to and say, "Amy I missed you."

Never ever will anyone replace Joannie. As a wife, as a lover, as a mom, or as a friend.

I know in my heart, in my spirit and in my dreams that she is smiling.

Joannie was selfless.

She redefined angels.

Having known her makes me smile.

chapter twenty-three

Amy

"My heart might be bruised, but it will recover and become capable of seeing beauty of life once more. It's happened before, it will happen again, I'm sure. When someone leaves, it's because someone else is about to arrive —I'll find love again."

~ Paulo Coelho, The Zahir

On three different occasions Joannie had said to me, "Keith, you are happier when you are married. I want you to find a remarkable woman after I'm gone. That is my hope for you."

I resisted at first but in my heart, I knew she was right. I did not what to live a life alone. I wanted to be in a relationship and to be married. I was a product of my parents which gave me a strong desire to raise a family with both a dad and a mom. Her unselfishness paved the way for Amy, who is now my wife.

The world is inhabited by angels. Those of us who are truly blessed are touched by one.

I have touched 'light and love' twice.

What a wonderful gift Joannie had given me. She was absolutely right about me. I love my wife, Amy, in every way. She is great with Andrew and Alex.

Joannie is smiling down upon us knowing that her boys are loved and are taken care of. Amy is their step-mom, loving the boys as her own.

The hugs that would have been hers are happily given by Amy and me.

I have found love again.

"The best kind of love is when you fall in love with the most unexpected person at the most unexpected time."

~ Unknown

Joannie had a small group of moms that she was especially close to. Judy is one of those precious women. About a year after Joannie's death I held a small barbeque and invited Judy, her husband John and several others to share the evening together. Judy and Joannie were always thick as thieves. Together our families enjoyed many back-yard parties, Easter dinners and impromptu get togethers.

They were like sisters, always laughing at some shared joke. Trading knowing smiles as they talked about their children.

On this summer evening Judy brought along a colleague from work.

Amy.

Wow. My heart skipped. The world stopped for a moment as I caught my breath.

During the evening I tried my best to spend time with everyone but found myself drifting to Amy's side. She was captivating. Warm. Honest and full of life.

Later I pulled Judy aside and asked … 'what is Amy's story?' Clearly, I was interested in her. Judy looked me in the eyes and said that Amy was single. I asked if she would be ok if I asked Amy for her number.

'No.'

'WHAT???'

'Keith, you are not ready. You are still grieving. Also, Amy is also grieving her divorce. Neither of you are ready.'

Who is Judy to tell me … 'NO.'

She is a trusted friend. I let it be, knowing that this angel, who was laughing in my back yard, would soon disappear from my life.

I let Amy go. I trusted Judy. Then again, she would hunt me down if I didn't listen to her!

Time passed. The fog slowly lifted.

The Courage to Embrace the Future

About a year later I was talking to Judy and I asked '…how is Amy?' She smiled 'We were just talking about you. Amy was wondering about you too.'

The next day, with phone number in hand I called Amy. I felt like a sixteen-year-old boy calling a girl he had a crush on. I was nervous. Courage grew as we spoke. Later we had lunch. Then dinner. With time we were dancing in one another's arms.

I fell in love all over again.

Her name is Amy, she is my sweetie pea.

I proposed within a year, and even traveled to Arizona to ask her dad for his blessing. Imagine, a 45-year-old man asking 'dad' for permission. Well I was brought up old school, good upbringing never failed me.

The first thing that Bill asked '… do you expect Amy to pay for your boys' college?' I was caught off guard. 'No. Absolutely not. I want to marry your daughter because I am in love with her and the boys adore her.'

He smiled and said 'yes.'

A Step Mother

I introduced Amy to the boys while we were dating. Well not immediately. I waited to be sure that she would be part of our life. I didn't want the boys get to know her, only to have her disappear from their lives.

That was not going to happen.

I proposed to Amy while we were all on a visit to my sister Astrid in the great Pacific Northwest. The boys were thrilled when we told them that we wanted to get married. Amy had spent enough time with Andrew and Alex to have made a great impression on them. I assured the boys that she would never replace their mother.

Amy was going to be my wife, and if they would have her ... she would be their step mom.

They did!

Fine Young Men

Amy is not just my sweetie pea, she is the stepmother for our boys. She is an active and guiding light in their lives. Today we are proud in how the boys have found love and honor what it means to be a man.

Today, Andrew and Alex are 23 and 22. They are happy, healthy and extraordinary people. For years the three of us were the 'three Amigos.'

A broken man with his two boys. Not great 'Amigos'.

Struggling along a path that we never expected. With each passing day the tears became fewer. The memories of Joannie, their mom, never far away.

With time, the pain shifted and was slowly replaced with a kind of understanding. Never acceptance. An acknowledgement that death is a scary reality. It was part of life.

But still disappointed at the injustice that their mom was dead.

The Future is Here

Andrew has finished college graduating as an engineer. He has started his career, has his own apartment and as many parents are happy to say … 'he is no longer on Dad's payroll!' He understands love and has found his soulmate. All I can do is smile knowing that this is all that his mom and I ever hoped for.

Andrew is here to find love and be the guiding hand in a wonderous family. I can't wait to be part of what he creates.

Alex has one more semester at college and he too will graduate as an engineer. I guess the apple really doesn't fall far from the tree. His path is yet to be defined, but he has a deep purpose that will be remarkable and unfold with time. Love is part of his path and we are honored to be part of it.

Alex is on this earth to experience life to its fullest. It will be remarkable, and I can't wait to hear all about it!

Our boys are still young. In their early twenties. Lives that are just beginning. Adventures to be had. Wonders to be appreciated.

I smile when I see them. Each time I hug them I hold on just a little longer so that their mom's love can touch them too. As I let go, I give them a quick kiss.

Yes, I am a sentimental old dad, but that is what I am, their mom and dad.

The boys are happy and so am I.

The Future is Now

Amy has helped me find my 'true North' and together we are breathing deeply of the air that gives us life.

We are there for one another in ways that I could never have imagined. Individually we have each overcome tremendous challenges. Together we look forward to the possibilities of what we are creating as a couple, ... as a family.

Life does go on. We will always be connected to those who have gone before us. We will honor them and strive to make them proud.

Today I have light in my life.

I am blessed to have Amy as my wife.

Together we look forward, while honoring our past.

chapter twenty-four

Reflections

*"Life can only be understood backwards;
but it must be lived forwards."*

~Søren Kierkegaard

As I look back on my life with Joannie, I realize today that it was an intense blend of married bliss, best friendship, romantic highs, challenging lows, incredible boys, the never ending loss of a daughter. Together we had the love of two extended families providing support, joy and poignancy and finally, a fatal disease that swept in like a terrorist in the night and took my love away forever.

All those things happened.

Before I met Joannie Lehman, none of those things had even entered on my radar scope. I had no idea.

That is the fickleness of life.

What you never expect becomes reality and then that reality is replaced by an unexpected new reality. We have little control over most of it despite our vain attempts to do so.

People come in and out of our lives like a destined revolving door and we barely have time to say goodbye to one before they are replaced by another. Just when we settle in with our new loves and soulmates it happens all over again.

Worse yet, there is never any pattern to all of this; it is just a set of random relationships and events that appear magically before our eyes and for our consideration.

With Joannie, I was blessed to the core of my being to have her in my life here on earth. Because our existence here is finite, I knew she and I would not last forever. I do believe in afterlife but that is something I choose to deal with later when that time comes.

So, it was inevitable that one of us would die and leave the other one to struggle through the pain of moving forward. I was sad it had to be her who passed away instead of me.

She had so much to give to the world. I was just an engineer who stayed in my career and family lane.

But today, I have been born again because of the woman I loved. I am now taking more risks, daring to try new things, reaching out to others and expanding my potential.

Joannie taught me that life has so much to offer and I have so much to give back. That is how she lived. That is how I want to be remembered when I die.

Rick Reynolds, a notable humorist, stated, "Death gives

meaning to life. Without death, there is no end. Because we all have a limited time here on earth, we need to value life as deeply as possible."

Thank you, death.

In her short years on earth, Joannie lived an incredible life. She was not cheated out of her existence. She accomplished her goals and realized her dream of marriage and a family.

She had touched everyone who came into contact with her and laughed and cried and enjoyed every emotion in her being.

By the time death came and got her, she had already won.

As I reflect on the remaining time on earth, that is exactly what I want to do, as well. I want to be Joannie. She is my role-model for how a human is supposed to behave in their lifetime.

To paraphrase the epic of Frank Sinatra's ballad, "*I want to do it my way and I am not going to wait until I am ready to die before I enjoy my reflections.*"

I want to live them now.

"Your past is done, so forget it. Your future is yet to come so dream it. But, your present is now so live it with no regrets."

chapter twenty-five
Life

*"The purpose of life is not to be happy.
It is to be useful, to be honorable, to be
compassionate, to have it make some difference
that you have lived and lived well."*

~Ralph Waldo Emerson

Your purpose on earth is determined by your philosophy of life.

If you are a Christian, it is to glorify God.
If you are an Atheist, it is to be all you can be to yourself.
If you are a Buddhist, it is to experience Nirvana.
If you are a Moslem, you want to always please Allah.
If you are a Jew, it is to live a healthy and holy life.
If you are a Hedonist, it is the unending pursuit of pleasure.
If you are a Moral individual, it is to do always what is right.

It just depends on who you are and what you believe.

I am a religious and spiritual hybrid who is open to many thoughts, ideas and beliefs. Therefore, my purpose in life is to always be an open-minded seeker of universal experiences.

We are here in this life, to experience what it means to be alive. To be part of something more than ourselves.

Each day is a gift. Each moment a brief insight to what is possible with intention.

As Joannie neared the last moments of her life, I saw that the flecks of time began to slow. Each moment, each breath lasted an eternity. As I held her hand with our boys at her side, I realized that the immensity of life is not in the last moments. It is in all that we experienced together. It was in the love that we shared. It is in what we will ultimately be together.

I never want to limit the possibilities of what might be happening out there.

I have no intention of tracking down flying saucers or preaching reincarnation, but I am always searching for what might be or could exist.

At my core, my purpose in life is to be true to who I am and always strive to do what is right, to not judge others and their beliefs, to consistently help those in need and to use my mind and talents to create inventive and powerful ways to make this world a better place.

My purpose is to be a leader, not a follower. I want to be an influencer; not a spectator.

There are three types of people in the world,

"Those that make things happen.
Those that watch things happen.
Those that say, 'what happened?'"

Like Joannie, I want to make things happen. I have committed my ideas, experiences, talents and career to that end. Life is too short to wait around letting others define my existence.

I want to be an "all or nothing" person. If I believe in it, I will do it will all my heart. If I don't, I won't.

There are a lot of other tentacles to this approach to life, but you get the idea.

I encourage you to discover your purpose on earth. It is a lot easier being yourself when you know who your self is in life. That way, you are not drifting to be manipulated by everyone else's opinion on how you should live.

As I said, "Life is too short."

To those that ask, 'how can I go on?"

Having been a breath away from death on many occasions I wonder *'How do we find peace after the loss of someone so special that we feel literally broken inside when they are gone?'*

This is a personal experience.

Everyone's loss is individual. Special. Unique. No one can

appreciate what we have lost.

No one. Ever.

Is it when we stop crying spontaneously every hour? Is it when you can sleep for more than three hours without the sudden lurch that wakes us up bringing back the flood of memories that define the daily horrors of watching some-one die? Does the passage of time that makes the pain a dull ache ok? What about the regrets, could I have done something else?

There are no words that can describe the pain that survivors go through, let alone endure. It is a personal and private journey that in the end is another of life's experiences.

Birth, growing up, falling in love, creating a family, seeing the fruits of our efforts and smiling as the sun slowly sets are what we are taught to expect.

Sometimes it just doesn't happen that way.

Our children die before us.

Parents pass before their children are old enough to stand on their own.

Our partners are taken well before their time.

For me there is no simple answer. Just as there is no agree-ment on why we are alive, why life is such a struggle and why those who deserve to live are taken so soon.

I do offer but one thing.

Life is to be lived. To be experienced.

Surround yourself with those who you honor and love. Be good to those who you encounter.

Accept that which you cannot control and appreciate that tomorrow will bring new possibilities. Try to be open to them.

This is not enough.

It will never be.

I know.

epilogue

My late wife was diagnosed with a terrible disease that ravaged her body and spirit for two years before finally taking her life. We worked tirelessly during those years to help her fight the disease and recover her health and life.

My boys and I accepted that my wife and their mother was ill, and that we would use every resource at our disposal to help and that we would work together to do anything and everything to help her survive.

What we failed to realize was that she was not the only one suffering. Andrew, Alex and I all suffered from emotional, physical, mental and spiritual stress as a result of the fatal diagnosis and it took everything from us as we tried desperately to help Joannie survive.

The suffering continued for the Lehman's and the Leust's. Together we were all a 'tribe.' Forever connected by Joannie.

The loss of Joannie has caused ripples across so many lives.

The suffering crept into the deepest fiber of our family, friends, moms and dads.

In the end, the effects of penetrating grief and pain, and yet hope for the future, affected each of us in different and very profound ways.

Now, years after Joannie's death, my boys and I are in a good place.

I realize now how 'broken' we all were, how much help we received and how fortunate we were to receive the much-needed support from our friends and family to help our own healing.

All these friends and family members have convinced me of two immutable truths:

- *first that life is to be lived in the fullest. Breath each day with renewed excitement and appreciate its promise.*

- *secondly, embrace what you have and be happy with the gifts bestowed upon you. After all, life is fleeting.*

They would have made Joannie smile.

I love you always,

Keith

April 2018

www.ingramcontent.com/pod-product-compliance
Lightning Source LLC
Chambersburg PA
CBHW031621040426
42452CB00007B/620